I0478641

PROJECT
MANAGEMENT
AT WORK

•PRACTICAL, RELEVANT RESULTS•

Dorcas M. T. Cox, MBA, PMP

iUniverse LLC
Bloomington

Project Management at Work
•PRACTICAL, RELEVANT RESULTS•

Copyright © 2013 Dorcas M. T. Cox, MBA, PMP.

All rights reserved. No part of this book may be used or reproduced by any means, graphic, electronic, or mechanical, including photocopying, recording, taping or by any information storage retrieval system without the written permission of the publisher except in the case of brief quotations embodied in critical articles and reviews.

iUniverse books may be ordered through booksellers or by contacting:

iUniverse
1663 Liberty Drive
Bloomington, IN 47403
www.iuniverse.com
1-800-Authors (1-800-288-4677)

Because of the dynamic nature of the Internet, any web addresses or links contained in this book may have changed since publication and may no longer be valid. The views expressed in this work are solely those of the author and do not necessarily reflect the views of the publisher, and the publisher hereby disclaims any responsibility for them.

Any people depicted in stock imagery provided by Thinkstock are models, and such images are being used for illustrative purposes only.

Certain stock imagery © Thinkstock.

ISBN: 978-1-4917-0281-9 (sc)
ISBN: 978-1-4917-0283-3 (hc)
ISBN: 978-1-4917-0282-6 (e)

Library of Congress Control Number: 2013914338

Printed in the United States of America.

iUniverse rev. date: 8/19/2013

Table of Contents

To my mother, Ena-mae T. Cox; Desiree Cox; and David Allens, as well as all others who dare to believe and have the courage to try.

Preface

I have applied my experience of more than eighteen years in human resources management, human resources development, organizational development, and project management throughout this book.

Born of the need for a practical, easy-to-understand guide for people with little or no prior experience in project management, this book may help to reduce the stress and anxiety that often accompany managing projects in the workplace. Each of the five chapters applies project management processes, from analyzing goals and identifying stakeholders to managing expectations, overcoming barriers to communication, and monitoring and evaluating progress and results.

As you read, you may find that the compelling saga around which the concepts are introduced mirrors familiar scenarios from your own firsthand experience. As you relate to the concepts and become engrossed in their application, you will find that many templates commonly used in project management are provided for you in a completed format, creating a simulated learning experience in which concepts are well anchored.

Prior to earning my Project Management Professional (PMP) designation from the Project Management Institute, I searched for books on project management. None of them married the inclusion of populated templates with an explanation of when and how these templates should be used in a way that I understood.

Over my many years of teaching project management certification classes, I have found that students lament that they read about input and output documents referenced in *A Guide to the Project Management Body of Knowledge (PMBOK Guide)* and have no idea what these input and output documents look like. Many students work in organizations where project management processes are not formalized. To assist in gaining this valuable understanding I have populated several commonly used templates that the *PMBOK Guide* references as input and corresponding output documents when completing certain project management processes and included these completed templates throughout this book. Feel free to use them on your respective projects. You will also find information on contract types that students find useful in everyday practice. I use *Project Management at Work* as a primary-source reference when teaching project management essentials and intermediate courses to continuing education students. I trust that you will find this book beneficial to you.

Introduction

Following proven project management techniques will help you develop greater skill in anticipating and addressing change and effectively communicating. You will learn to go beyond the theory of applying project management processes; moving instead to becoming aware of and adjusting to workplace culture, norms, and practices. Securing buy-in and clarifying expectations along the way are also key to managing projects in ways that improve employee and business outcomes.

This book instructs you to flesh out concepts and crystallize ideas in ways that promote broad thinking, considering the variables that may impact possible outcomes. When used at the outset, project-initiating processes may provide valuable information to determine the viability of proceeding to the next steps in the process.

Who Should Read This Book

Project Management at Work is intended to captivate the interest of persons who are

- new to the field of project management,
- members of project teams,
- required to execute projects in accordance with a project plan,
- aspiring to attain roles with increasing responsibilities that include and are not limited to project management,
- focusing on real-world practical application of project management, or
- increasing their breadth and depth of project management knowledge.

As an in-depth training manual, this book should be interesting and useful for those wishing to develop and hone their project management skills. The fictional story woven through the text makes the narrative compelling and aids in instructional illustration to promote efficiency in absorbing content.

How to Read This Book

Project Management at Work is written in a way that allows the reader to cover the book sequentially or skip to chapters that address their specific concerns. Chapters contain completed templates and expert tips that help you to increase knowledge, skill, and confidence, avoid mistakes, save time and money, and increase productivity.

Chapter 1

Initiate Your Project

After studying this chapter, you should be able to accomplish the following:

- give the definition of a project
- differentiate between projects, programs, and portfolios
- differentiate between functional, matrix, and projectized organizational structures
- define and explain the importance of project initiation
- state what happens if some of the steps in project initiation are left out
- list and describe the steps to be taken as a part of project initiation
- define stakeholders and list the persons and/or groups—internal and/or external to the organization—that fit that definition
- describe the importance of stakeholders
- explain the importance of properly identifying stakeholders at the outset of the project

---

"Next stop, Kings Cross Station." The monotonous sound of the conductor's recorded voice jolts David from his nap with sudden awareness that his stop is next.

David arches backward in his seat, cups his hands behind his neck, and yawns openly. His is young and enthusiastic about moving up in the organization, but his progress up the corporate ladder appears slow in his estimation.

The company is built on core values and guiding principles. It promotes from within and prides itself on embracing diversity and adding value by giving back to the community. That's what attracted David to join ten years ago as an assistant manager. But he is still just a manager now, so many years later.

Maybe he should have done a better job at networking, building relationships with the people who are going places and being visible.

"Be a shameless self-promoter," one of the movers and shakers told David. That's what it takes to move ahead nowadays, especially in an organization where there is reliance on the immediate manager for promotion endorsement. Clearly David needs a mentor.

The train slows to a jolting stop; the doors open. David hustles out along with hundreds of morning commuters on the procession to work. As he walks the three last blocks to the office, David anticipates what lies ahead in the coming weeks in his new role as project manager. It's no promotion, *just a lateral move with no change in level or pay,* he reminds himself, citing verbatim from the letter received from human resources. He was seriously considering turning down the offer for the twelve-month temporary transfer to the project team. Someone else would backfill his job. He would sink or swim. Success may mean a promotion. Failure will mean that he's a "floater" moving from one cubicle to the next, with no real desk, just filling in for people on leave.

Why take the plunge into project management?

"What's in it for me?" he asks, canvassing opinions from trusted friends and colleagues over whether or not he should accept the offer.

Most of them say, "You'll see another side of the business; you'll grow, expand, and learn."

All of that sounded good, but the thing that really sealed the deal and convinced him to accept the offer was the notion that the new assignment would, at the very least, temporarily relieve the monotonous routine of his teensy weensy job, which he'd outgrown years ago. He would exceed expectations even in a semicomatose state, the state that he typically operated in every boring day of his work life. And if just for the notion that for once he could be alive at work, he was willing to take the chance to move from complement to overrun status on the organization chart, relegated to floating after the project is over as a reward.

Look at the time; pick up the pace; can't let this elevator go. I'll be late! Elbowing his way into the crowded elevator, he presses the button to the twentieth floor, stopping at floors like a game of speed chess where players hit the clock to signal the start and end of a play. Twentieth floor, match over. The game has just begun.

Projects, Programs and Portfolios

Day planner, notebook, and pen in hand, David makes his way toward the boss's office for a briefing on the project requirements. When he arrives, his boss greets him and explains that the organization is embarking on several projects to realize strategic objectives in the coming fiscal year. Some projects reside in portfolios; others are included in programs based on their relationship to the organization's strategy. The portfolio that the boss manages includes a collection of projects and programs. Grouped within the portfolio are programs comprised of subprograms, projects, or other work managed in a coordinated fashion to support the portfolio.

At the boss's prompt for questions, David voices his concern: "I'm concerned about reporting and my level of authority, given that my role of project manager involves sourcing skills and expertise from persons senior to me. These persons are assigned to different departments and projects in business lines where I have no authority. Over the last ten years of working with the company I know full well that the power base lies in the hands of the functional department head. One too many times I made the mistake of going directly to an employee in production or marketing without first routing the request through the functional department head only to be hauled before my boss on charges of breach of the chain of command. I was admonished on several occasions to know my role or I would soon find myself on the outside looking in, which may explain why I've only moved up one level in the organization after ten consecutive years of employment. But that's another story."

"Interesting. Your impression is that this organization structure is functional?" The boss is curt. "In reality this organization uses a balanced matrix structure. Balanced matrix structures blend functional and projectized characteristics."

"Balanced matrix structures, projectized characteristics? Please explain," David requests, his brow furrowed. "These concepts are still rather new to me."

"No worries," the boss replies. "A functional organization is probably the oldest type of organization. Functional organizations are grouped according to functions; for example, an organization may have human resources, purchasing, and accounting departments. The work in these departments is specialized and requires people whose skill sets relate to that function to carry out the work of the department. This type of organization is set up to be a hierarchy," the boss explains. "Employees report to supervisors who report to managers reporting to department heads who report to the organization's head. Ultimately, one person at the top is in charge. Are you with me?" the boss inquires without preamble.

"Yes, I'm following you so far."

"Many companies today, including governmental organizations, are structured in a hierarchical fashion." Reclining misty-eyed in his chair, the boss's eyes transfix on his wall art, appearing to peer into past years in organizations similar to that which he describes. "Be aware of the chain of command!" he states with jolting exclamation.

"You mean don't talk to the big boss before talking to your boss who talks to their boss who talks to the big boss?"

"You got it. Each department or group in a functional organization is managed independently, with a limited span of control. Human resources does not run purchasing or its projects, for example. Human resources is concerned with their own functions and projects. If it is necessary for human resources to get input from purchasing on a project, the human resources team follows the chain of command."

To David it appears that the words "follow the chain of command" are uttered with a hint of sternness; it may be his imagination.

"The human resources manager speaks with the purchasing manager, getting the necessary information to pass on to the project team. Projectized organizations are pretty much the reverse of functional organizations. The focus of these organizations is the project itself. In a projectized organization, the loyalty is to the project, not the functional manager. In these organizations project managers have ultimate control over the project, reporting directly to the top boss."

"Are organizational resources dedicated to the project work in these organizations?"

"Yes. In a purely projectized organization, functions such as human resources and purchasing, for example, may report directly to the project manager. Project managers make decisions that relate to the project while acquiring and assigning resources, hiring from within or outside of the organization."

"What about the matrix organization? That is a new term to me—before today I never knew that such an organizational structure existed."

"Matrix organizations are somewhat of a hybrid. The better aspects of two organizational structures are combined into one. Employees in a matrix organization report to one functional manager and at least one project manager. Functional managers assign employees to projects and monitor their employees' work on various projects. Project managers, like you, David, execute the project and distribute work assignments according to project activities, and both the project manager and the functional manager share responsibility for completing the employee's performance review. In a balanced matrix organization, the power is balanced between functional managers and project managers. Each manager is responsible for their aspect of the project or organization. The employee is assigned to projects based on the project needs, not because the project manager or functional manager used the heavy-handed approach to acquire or retain the best resources, as the case may be.

"The classification of a balanced matrix is based on the level of power and influence between functional and project managers. In the balanced matrix the project manager shares the authority and power to make decisions with the functional manager. This means that although your job level is manager and you may be requesting information and support from senior managers, you have clout and they will honor your request, the same as they would if you were their immediate boss."

"I get it," David replies, understanding the concepts better after the boss's clarification.

"Apologies for dashing off to another meeting," the boss mumbles.

He is distracted, hurriedly pulling papers together from all angles of his desk. He refers David to the shared drive where the repository of project plans, processes, policies, and procedures specific to the organization resides. The information in the shared drive is used to perform and govern the project. The boss suggests that David take the remainder of the week to look at completed schedules, lessons learned, historical information, risk data, and earned-value data, not to mention human resources policies such as health and safety, ethics, and project management. He would also need to review information on project and product life cycles and quality policies and procedures, including process audits, improvement targets, checklists, and standardization process definitions used in the organization.

"Oh yes," the boss declares. "There's lots to keep you busy until the end of the week. My calendar is usually up-to-date. See when I'm free in the beginning of next week and send me an invite. Sorry to have to cut this meeting short. Welcome aboard; it's great having you." With that, the boss is gone.

David realizes that he needs formal project management training and a mentor/coach to navigate the balanced matrix organization structure that the boss describes. He has never been good at building relationships or networking; he doesn't have the components in his arsenal to strategically influence key decision makers.

Luckily the company's learning management system includes an online project management class, and David doesn't waste any time: he enters his employee ID, user name, and password to register for the class. He sees that assignment to a mentor/coach is required upon registration, and he signs up for one.

The first lesson is called "Module 1: Project Initiation." At the prompt, David launches the self-study course, downloads the self-study materials, and immerses himself in the learning content.

The module defines a project as a temporary endeavor. The end is reached when the project's objectives are achieved or when the project is terminated because its objectives will not or cannot be met, or when the need for the project no longer exists. The module goes on to explain that projects come about to produce a tangible or intangible unique product, service, or result.

David's interest is piqued as begins to read about the difference between portfolios and programs. The module talks about the same thing that he recalls his boss saying about a portfolio as a collection of projects and programs that are managed as a group. According to the boss, the project that David will manage is included as a part of a portfolio. The organization's strategic objective is the link between projects, programs, and portfolios. Projects are prioritized based on risk, funding, resources, and other considerations that support achieving the organization's strategic plan.

Reluctantly, David takes a stab at completing the practice activity. He's really not in the mood to read and complete a case scenario; at the same time, he needs to submit something to his mentor/coach for review and discussion during the one-on-one session.

Activity #1—Practical Application of Relationship between Projects, Programs, and Portfolios

The practical application of determining the relationship between projects, programs, and portfolios is presented in the form of a case scenario.

Instructions
1. Read the case scenario: "Believe You Can: Healthy Solutions."
2. Write down what projects, programs, or portfolios you recommend based on the information presented.
3. Include the rationale for your decision.
4. Jot down any questions you may have.
5. Discuss your decision with the mentor/coach assigned to your program.

Case Scenario
Believe You Can: Healthy Solutions has been in business for the past fifty consecutive years and is a leader in the health and wellness industry.

The company operates out of four state-of-the-art production locations where it manufactures educational books, magazines, and CDs. The newest production facility currently operates at only 50 percent of production capacity. The company also offers classes, workshops, and online/face-to-face membership support groups facilitated by certified counselors. Believe You Can: Healthy Solutions has a staff of over three hundred permanent employees. Its business model focuses on external sales, on-site delivery, and a loyalty strategy.

Key Buyers (Who the Company Is Selling Products/Services to)
- book sellers (50 percent of sales), health centers/gyms (25 percent of sales), and civic organizations/community groups (25 percent of sales)—percentages obtained from end-of-year product sales in the youth and adult market (male and female)

Products and Services (What the Company Is Selling)
- books (50 percent of sales), magazines (30 percent of sales), CDs (3 percent of sales), classes/workshops (5 percent of sales), membership online support groups (2 percent of sales), and membership face-to-face support groups (10 percent of sales)—percentages obtained from end-of-year total product sales in the youth and adult market (male and female)

Key Resources/Activities
- networking/referrals, brand awareness, and expertise

Key Activities
- relationship-focused selling to buyers
- upgrading educational material based on customer and market research feedback
- upgrading marketing and sales strategy
- establishing a loyalty program
- generating referrals

Channels
- direct marketing (external sales strategy)
- awareness through marketing/public relations materials
- on-site delivery and postpurchase customer support
- online delivery options

Current-Year Target
- build market share in niche market, senior citizen (sixty- to eighty-five-year-old male and female)
- build brand recognition as the de-facto leader in designing, developing, and distributing materials that promote healthy lifestyles
- realize total gross sales of two million from sales of products in senior citizen niche market by end of current fiscal year
- manage expenses to no more than 6 percent of gross sales

What projects, programs, or portfolios would you recommend based on the information presented below?

David gives up fifteen minutes into completing the case scenario, opens up a chat, and starts sending and checking e-mails. He smiles as he messages a buddy from his old department who is jabbing at him for moving up the corporate ladder. Sadly, he confesses, he may be returning to the old job sooner than expected. He's not sure that he's fitting into the new environment. He doesn't feel connected, his boss sent him to review material on the shared drive with no direction, he's trying to teach himself by completing an online module, and he has no idea where to begin, so he is giving up and thinking about heading off for an early extended lunch. After he hits the send button his cell phone rings. His buddy talks him down off the ledge.

Together they work through each of the case study questions. One and a half hours later David is done typing and sends the response below to his mentor/coach for review and discussion. With a sense of accomplishment and renewed enthusiasm toward the job, David heads to lunch with pep in his step and a smirk on his face. He feels good about himself. Things are progressing.

1. Products and Services (What the Company Is Selling)

Product	Percent of Sales
Books	50 percent
Magazines	30 percent
CDs	3 percent
Classes/Workshops	5 percent
Membership Face-to-Face Support Groups	10 percent

* These percentages are obtained from end-of-year total product sales in the youth and adult market (male and female).

2. Key Buyers (Who the Company Is Selling To)

Major Customers	Percent of Total Sales
Book Sellers	50 percent
Health Centers/Gyms	25 percent
Civic Organizations/Community	25 percent

* These percentages are obtained from end of year product sales in the youth and adult market (male and female).

	Yes	No
3. Is production at or near capacity?		X

4. Describe the Selling Process
- o relationship-focused selling to suppliers/buyers
- o direct marketing (external sales strategy)
- o awareness through marketing/public relationship materials
- o on-site delivery and postpurchase customer support
- o online delivery options
- o generating referrals
- o establishing loyalty program

5. **Targeted Customer Groups for Futures Sales Growth**
   o   senior citizens (sixty to eighty-five years old), male and female

6. **Is the health and wellness industry new, growing, mature, or declining?**
   o   mature

7. **Is the competition new, growing, mature, or declining?**
   o   all

8. **Is the business new, growing, mature, or declining?**
   o   growing/mature

9. **What is the business relying on to make their product or service superior to the competition?**
   o   quality reputation, experience, and solid financial performance

10. **What are the key factors for the success of the new product line?**
    o   industry expertise
    o   established selling process
    o   brand/name recognition
    o   loyalty through life stages

Possible Recommendations

1. Project to create additional face-to-face membership support groups for niche market in locations where the service is currently offered.
2. Project to create marketing and promotional campaign/ advertising. Use affiliates in doctor's office, gyms, and food manufacturers.
3. Project to create a new magazine line to cater to niche market.
4. Project to increase production capacity.

Projects 1, 2, and 3 combine to create a program.
Projects 1, 2, 3, and 4 combine to create a portfolio.

When David has been back from lunch for a few minutes who should appear? You guessed it—the boss, this time sporting the biggest grin ever, a far cry from the preoccupied state David recalls from the morning briefing.

"How's it going?" is the familiar greeting.

"It's going. I'm working on an online module and e-mailed the assignment to my mentor/coach just before lunch."

"Yeah, so I understand. That's why I'm here. You really did a great job on it. Very thorough, detailed; obviously a lot of work went into it. Great job!"

"Thanks," David replies cautiously. *How connected is the boss?* David just sent the e-mail to his mentor/coach one hour ago. *Surely this guy is not just shooting the breeze; his presence typically translates into something strategic.*

"So, what's the next step?"

"Time is short. The beginning of the fiscal year is just days away. We're shooting for tight turnaround times for you to have this project completed and rolled out. Bonuses depend on this success … yours and mine. Finish those online modules on your own time. I need to have the project charter and stakeholder register signed off by the end of this week. With these documents in hand we can see that proceeding to design, develop, and delivery of the initiative is the next step. Additionally, based on the research that we've done, the probability of this project succeeding is high."

David gets the hint as the boss pauses and looks directly at him. He makes the next move.

"Well. Then I'll begin working on the project charter," he replies with fake enthusiasm.

"Yes, of course. The project charter is the written acknowledgment that the project exists. We need this document to name you as project manager and to authorize assigning resources to this project. I'll discuss this matter with the vice president and the chief executive officer this afternoon after our meeting and schedule them to sign off on the charter and stakeholder register by the end of this week. I need your commitment to have the project charter on my desk by the end of the business day tomorrow. I'm off to my meeting. We'll chat later."

With that, the boss whisks off, faster than a speeding bullet into corporate superhero world.

The Charter

With no experience writing either a project charter or a stakeholder register, David nevertheless keenly takes a stab at creating both documents authorizing the project work and identifying the stakeholders. The boss is busy arranging the vice president and the chief executive officer's sign-off on both documents at the end of the week.

The project charter authorizes the project and David as project manager to apply resources. While some source documents necessary to prepare the project charter include the project statement of work, a business case, and a contract, the nature of the project drives the documents for actual use. For example, a contract may only be necessary when an aspect of the project work is performed by external vendors, as is the case in the project that David manages. In this instance, the information that David needs from the contract for inclusion in the charter may include the conditions under which the project will be executed, the anticipated time frame, and a description of the work.

David reviews the business case for the current fiscal year with forensic detail. He analyzes the business, which was created based on the market demand and organizational need as the impetus for initiating the project. He also peruses the cost/benefit analysis created as justification for the project.

For the aspects of the project work performed internal to the organization, David reviews a project statement of work, obtaining a description of the product, service, or result that the project is undertaken to complete, the business need, the product scope description, and other strategic related information.

Another crucial consideration when documenting the project charter is the external and internal environment in which the project operates. David reviews source documents providing him with insight into the organizational culture, government or industry standards, the political climate, and the organization's policies, procedures, and guidelines for conducting project-related work.

Sample Project Charter

Project Title:	JJ Enterprises Records Management

Project Sponsor:	Jason and Jamina McKenzie	**Date Prepared:**	June 20XX
Project Manager:	John Doe	**Project Customer:**	JJ Enterprises

Project Purpose or Justification:

JJ Enterprises is a locally owned and operated fast-food restaurant that has been in business for the past three years. The company's rapid expansion resulted in records with no clear filing arrangement.

Project Description:

Revamp the records management and filing system presently in place for JJ Enterprises' fifteen locations.

High-Level Project and Product Requirements:

- Conduct a needs analysis determining the nature and purpose of records created in JJ Enterprises.
- Review the records practices currently being used in JJ Enterprises.
- Review the need for more human resources in the area of records management and make appropriate recommendation if necessary based on the proposed records management and filing arrangement.
- Create a design document of the records management system that is recommended to address deficiencies in the present system.
- Ensure that the classification system that is recommended for implementation is appropriate for the people who will be accessing the records.
- Consider the possibility of expansion at JJ Enterprises given that the records management and filing arrangement must be flexible for expansion as JJ Enterprises continues to grow.
- Recommend an appropriate filing arrangement to senior management that ensures that records are retrieved when needed.
- Develop the required indexes based on the filing arrangement.
- Implement a new records management system.
- Conduct training sessions for records management staff on the use of the system.
- Roll out a system implementation with opportunities for feedback.
- Conduct an evaluation, including measurement of records management staff reaction.
- Develop a maintenance plan.

Summary Budget:

Project costs US$30,000.

Initial Risks:

- Jason and Jamina may not be receptive to changes accompanying the recommendations.
- The records management staff may be unwilling to change old behaviors.
- The records management staff may revert to old behaviors after the project has been completed and integrated with the daily operations.
- The records management staff may feel threatened by the change.
- The records management staff may not be monitored after the project transitions into operations, and as such they may not adhere to the records management requirements as intended.
- It may be difficult to gain access to the records in the organization given the different locations.
- The learning curve with the records management staff may result in lower initial productivity.
- Some stakeholders may undermine or work against the project.
- The budget may be unrealistic.
- Employees may be confused with the new processes, which will affect their ability to utilize the solution.
- It is possible that new processes may not be fully integrated at first.
- Substantial change in processes may result in destructive behavior.
- Uncertainty may cause delay in decision making.
- It may be difficult to reach a consensus.

Summary Milestones	Due Date
• Conduct a needs analysis to determine the kinds of records that are being created in JJ Enterprises and their purpose.	June 4, 20XX
• Review the records practices currently being used in JJ Enterprises.	June 14, 20XX
• Review the need for more human resources in the area of records management and make appropriate recommendation if necessary based on the proposed records management and filing arrangement.	June 14, 20XX

• Complete project-initiating documents including project charter and stakeholder register.	June 14, 20XX
• Sign off on the project plan inclusive of subsidiary plans.	June 17, 20XX
• Create a design document of the records management system recommended to address deficiencies in the present system.	June 17, 20XX
• Sign off on design document for records management system.	June 17, 20XX
• Begin to produce project-executing and monitoring and controlling documents.	June 20, 20XX
• Ensure that the classification system recommended for implementation is appropriate for the people who will access the records.	June 21, 20XX
• Consider the possibility of expansion at JJ Enterprises given that the records management and filing arrangement must be flexible for expansion as JJ Enterprises continues to grow.	June 21, 20XX
• Recommend an appropriate filing arrangement that ensures that records are retrieved when needed.	June 22, 20XX
• Conduct roll out of records management system with corresponding training for records management staff.	June 23, 20XX
• Complete project close out, including lessons learned and integration into operations and implementation of maintenance plan.	June 24, 20XX

Project Objectives	Success Criteria	Person Approving
Scope:		
Revamp the records management and filing system presently in place for JJ Enterprises' fifteen locations.	Project scope success is achieved if the project remains within scope as defined in the corresponding project objectives.	• Project sponsor • Project manager

Time:

The integrity of the project schedule baseline must be upheld to ensure that the project has been completed and handed over to operations at JJ Enterprises within the deadline date.	The milestone schedule outlines the specific dates that must be met to determine schedule success.	• Project sponsor • Project manager

Cost:

The project cost is captured in terms of US$30,000.	Budgetary success is determined by achieving the objective of not exceeding US$30,000.	• Project sponsor • Project manager

Quality:

The product (records management system) must be produced in keeping with industry standards for records management/filing systems. The project must adhere to the project management standards outlined in the current edition of the *PMBOK Guide* established by the Project Management Institute.	The specific measurements that must be met for the project to be considered a success are included in the quality description in the corresponding column on the left.	• Project sponsor • Project manager

Acceptance Criteria:

The criteria outlined in the respective project documents must be met and accepted by the project sponsor.

Project Manager Authority Level

Staffing Decisions:

The project manager has the authority to hire, fire, discipline, accept, or not accept project staff.

Budget Management and Variance:

> The project manager has the authority to manage control and be accountable for the project funds. Project funding is not to exceed the amount of US$30,000.

Technical Decisions:

> The project manager has the authority to make technical decisions about the deliverables or the project approach.

Conflict Resolution:

> The project manager has the authority to resolve conflict within the team and with external stakeholders.

Escalation Path for Authority Limitations:

> Issues outside the authority level of the project manager should be escalated to the project sponsor.

Approvals:

_____	_____
Project Manager Signature	Sponsor or Originator Signature
_____	_____
Project Manager Name	Sponsor or Originator Name
_____	_____
Date	Date

David finds writing a project charter to be time consuming and taxing. In his case, perhaps the length of time taken to write the document can be attributed to a learning curve. On the other hand, the level of research and detailed accuracy required to properly complete the document takes time. Project charters are created to document the project-initiation process for the following reasons:

- The project charter will be used as an input to create the project plan.
- Information presented in the project charter is further elaborated on in the project plan. In other words, the project charter document serves as a primary guide for creating the project plan.

- The project charter details *what* will be done, and the project plan is the document that outlines *how* it will be done.
- The project charter outlines what is in and out of scope for the project. For example, if you are designing and developing a training program with an e-learning component and your project charter clearly states that creating the interface and programming modules are out of scope, this means that these services will not be provided in the context of this project this time.
- Key information in the project charter serves as a guide when creating the project plan and helps to provide some structure, ensuring that the resources are concentrated on what is in scope for the project.
- The project plan is mapped to the project charter, ensuring that the critical milestones that were agreed to and signed off on in the charter document are achieved within budget. The persons identified as responsible for certain roles are aware of their responsibilities and the estimated time that they should expect to invest to complete their responsibilities.
- The charter document should be sufficiently detailed, giving the sponsor (the person financing the initiative) a clear understanding of what he or she is authorizing.
- Input from stakeholders is included when creating the project charter given that stakeholders have something to gain or lose by the success or failure of the initiative.

Identify Stakeholders

It's dark outside, incandescent lights on a timer dim automatically, computers power down, and there's stillness. David takes a breath on his way to enjoy a social outing.

Work on developing stronger networking and relationship-building skills, he tells himself, pushing open the doors to the popular restaurant and lounge. For the first time he's agreed to join colleagues for an after-work social event. He needs to appear approachable and open some communication lines or at the very least make some friends. He's felt so lonely at work recently. No time for socializing—he must meet looming deadlines.

"Just two hours to socialize," he mumbles semiaudibly. "I have to finish writing the stakeholder register by tomorrow."

The evening progresses, and David openly displays his emotions. He's casual with his coworkers and talks about his project and the future with intuitive visions and outspoken spontaneity. His imagination and creativity draw others to him.

As David's status changes from outsider to insider he learns from the informal leaders in the department. He becomes aware of the group's communication patterns and is introduced to the group's language. David is advised that the stakeholder register that he began creating by reviewing the corporate directory, reviewing previous stakeholder registers from similar projects, and reading previous project documents is not as comprehensive as he had thought. Some stakeholders are missing from his list such as suppliers, contractors and the training manager. Key stakeholders are socializing nearby who have a vested interest in the outcome of the project and the ability to influence project results. They have something to either gain or lose as a result of the project's success or failure.

Immersed as a member of the department's informal and formal group, David is conscious of his role as a newcomer, and he plays it well. The formal and informal group is cohesive, and David feels acceptance. With a strong sense of belonging, his self-esteem elevates.

Before moving on to the next chapter, take time to complete the discussion questions to understand how the information presented in this chapter may be applied to the next project.

Key Points to Remember

- A project may be defined as a temporary initiative that has a clear start date and clear finish date; produces a unique product, service, or result; and is developed in greater detail as the work progresses.
- Using a standard method does not imply that you will not produce a unique outcome.
- Programs are groups of related projects managed using the same techniques in a coordinated fashion.
- Managing projects collectively as programs makes it possible to capitalize on benefits that would not be achievable if the projects were managed separately.

- Portfolios are a collection of programs and projects that support business goals and objectives.
- Portfolio, program, and project management are aligned with or driven by organizational strategies.
- Organizational strategy should provide guidance and direction to project management.
- An organization's culture and style affect how it conducts projects. Organizational culture is shaped by the common experiences of its members.
- A functional organization is a hierarchy where each employee has one clear manager or supervisor.
- The focus of projectized organizations is the project itself. Organizational resources are dedicated to the project and the project work, with the project manager having a great deal of independence and authority.
- Matrix organizations employ a blend of functional and projectized characteristics and are classified as weak, balanced, and strong depending on the relative level of power and influence between functional and project managers.
- Employees in a matrix organization report to one functional manager and at least one project manager. It is possible for employees to report to multiple project managers if they are working on more than one project at a time.
- In a matrix organization the functional managers ensure that the employee completes relative tasks as outlined in their position description according to their job title, job level, and performance objectives and development plan requirements for the fiscal year. They also monitor the work that their employee is performing on a particular project.
- In a matrix organization the project manager executes the project and distributes work assignments based on project activities. Project managers and functional managers share the responsibility of performance reviews for the employee in a matrix organization.

- Initiating a project officially authorizes a project, assigns a project manager, identifies the project stakeholders, and obtains the organization's commitment to the project.

- Initiating a project includes creating a project charter document and identifying stakeholders.
- A contract may only be necessary when the organization that you are working for is performing a project for a customer outside of the organization.
- A statement of work may be used when a contract is not available or is not necessary because the work being performed is internal to the organization.
- Stakeholders are people or organizations with a vested interest in the project. They are actively involved in the project with something to gain or lose by the project's success or failure.
- Identifying stakeholders is an ongoing process.
- The stakeholder register is the document that is used to identify those people and organizations impacted by the project.
- It is important that the project manager knows how to analyze stakeholders.
- The project manager must demonstrate advanced communication skills.

Applying to the Next Project

Discussion Questions

1. What is a project?
2. Why do organizations undertake projects?
3. How can projects be used for personal and community development?
4. What are some examples of project ideas for personal and community development?
5. What is a program?
6. What is a portfolio?
7. Why are projects, programs, and portfolios managed differently?
8. What is the difference between functional, matrix, and projectized organizational structures?
9. What are the advantages and disadvantages associated with functional, matrix, and projectized organizational structures?

10. What is meant by project initiation?
11. Why is project initiation important?
12. What documents are produced as a part of project initiation?
13. Who is responsible for producing project-initiation documents?
14. Who are the persons or groups internal or external to the organization that fit the definition of a stakeholder?
15. Why are stakeholders important?
16. Why is it important to properly identify stakeholders and compile an accurate stakeholder list at the outset of the project?
17. What happens if important information is omitted from project-initiation documents?
18. What does it mean when project-initiation documents are signed? What happens next?

Debrief Questions

1. What are the key learning points?
2. What information was new to you?
3. What concepts will you apply in the future? When?
4. What challenges do you anticipate may limit your ability to apply the concepts?
5. What needs to be in place to overcome these challenges?
6. Who would you recommend these concepts to and why?

Activity

The following activity may be completed individually or in a small group to assess your comprehension.

1. Answer the discussion questions.
2. Answer the debrief questions.
3. Use the completed templates presented in the chapter to create project-initiation documents for a project of your own.
4. Review previous projects where accurate stakeholder lists were not compiled and discuss the outcome in those instances.

Sample Stakeholder Register

Project Title: JJ Enterprises Records Management   **Date Prepared:**   June 20XX

Name	Position	Role	Contact Information	Requirements	Expectations	Influence	Classification
Jason and Jamina McKenzie	President and CEO	Support the application of knowledge and skill	Via contact listing	• have high-level understanding of program administration, execution, and value	• experience positive results reinforce concepts when project is integrated into operations • support all components of the program	High	Sponsor
Records management staff	Employees	Provide expert information, endorse initiative, and support use of knowledge and skills	Via contact listing	• possess technical skills • have high level of knowledge and skill as it relates to program administration and execution	• experience positive results • support all components of the program	High	Internal customer
Staff at JJ Enterprises	Employees	Support the application of knowledge and skill	Via contact listing	• have high-level understanding of program administration, execution, and value	• support all components of the program	High	Internal customer

Name	Position	Role	Contact Information	Requirements	Expectations	Influence	Classification
The project team	Vendor	Provide expert information. Endorse initiative and support use of knowledge and skills	Via contact listing	• have high-level understanding of program administration, execution, and value • possess knowledge and skill in project management as well as demonstrated ability to create and execute an effective project management plan • ensure that project remains in scope • adhere to project schedule milestone dates • ensure that project remains in budget • adhere to project quality measures	• experience positive results	High	Supplier

Chapter 2

Make a Plan

After studying this chapter, you should be able to accomplish the following:

- state the role of the project manager
- discuss the importance of the project manager
- define the purpose of the project-plan document
- explain what a project manager needs to know and what behavioral skills he or she should demonstrate
- summarize how a project manager applies knowledge and skills in and out of project settings
- list and describe eighteen steps to planning a project
- list and describe the purpose of some subsidiary documents that may be included in the project plan
- explain the purpose of a baseline
- explain why it is necessary to address all components of the planning process before deciding which processes are necessary to be completed based on the nature and scope of the project
- describe why it is necessary to revisit one or more planning processes throughout the life of the project
- outline the importance of collecting requirements
- list and describe ways to collect requirements
- describe what is included in or excluded from the project
- explain the steps in creating the work-breakdown structure (WBS)
- list all activities in each work package
- sequence all activities in each work package
- figure out which resources are needed to complete each activity

- determine how long it will take to complete the work associated with each activity
- schedule time to complete each activity
- estimate how much it would cost to complete each activity included as a part of a work package
- determine the budget for the project
- state why quality is important in a project
- describe the process for determining quality
- explain what may happen if some steps for assuring quality are missed
- list and describe some steps that may be followed to ensure quality
- describe why it is important to plan for your human resources
- explain the process of assigning the right people to complete each activity
- summarize what may happen if there is no plan to get people on and off the project
- define a communication plan
- explain the importance of a communication plan
- indicate what may happen in the absence of effective communication
- identify risks that may present themselves in a project
- describe some project documents that may be used to assist in identifying project risks
- discuss the methods that may be used to identify risks in a project
- list and describe the strategies for addressing negative risks or threats and positive risks or opportunities
- define procurements
- give examples of when it may be necessary to procure items on a project
- list and describe some project documents that may be used for information when determining procurement needs
- explain some considerations that may be addressed when planning procurements

- state the three different types of contracts that may be considered when planning procurements
- define what is meant by managing stakeholders

A shrill alarm and a flashing red light on his cell phone remind David of his scheduled appointment with his mentor/coach. He's running late. He has coffee in hand and bags under his eyes—another day at the office. The long hours needed to move the project along at warp speed are taking their toll. The first order of business is to arrange some time off next month.

The meeting begins with positive energy emitting from his mentor/coach as the motivator, affectionately referred to as the owl. The owl has been around for a long time. As a professor emeritus from the School of Hard Knocks, it's rumored that the owl has been pretty much everywhere and has seen it all.

The owl is determined and direct in initiating the dialogue.

"When you think about the role of the project manager," she declares, "the first thing that comes to mind shouldn't be a red carpet walk to receive the PEMMY award for the role of lead actor in a project management drama or for role of best supporting actress in a project suspense thriller. At the same time, there are roles, a set of connected behaviors, and obligations that you should demonstrate in certain situations as project manager."

"As project manager," she continues, stretching her crane-like neck, "you will often be required to play multiple roles. You may be a guide, an influencer, a consensus builder, an observer, a peacemaker, a taskmaster, an empathetic listener, an encourager, or a documenter based on the situation.

Guide
"As a guide, you must know the steps in the process from beginning to end and carefully guide your project team, customers, and stakeholders through each phase in the project life cycle.

Influencer

"As an influencer, you must ignite enthusiasm in your team and stakeholder group as you establish momentum for your project and keep the team on pace.

Consensus Builder

"As a consensus builder, you must find ways to establish an environment conducive to building consensus.

Observer

"In your role of observer, you must watch carefully for potential signs of strain, frustration, and resistance from members of the stakeholder group and your project team.

Peacemaker

"As a peacemaker, you must move quickly to effectively restore order and direct your team toward constructive resolution when conflict arises.

Taskmaster

"As a taskmaster, you are ultimately responsible for keeping your project team on track and managing the various processes on the project.

Empathetic Listener

"As an empathetic listener, you must listen carefully to understand the meaning of and relate to what is being said.

Encourager

"As an encourager, you must praise effort and achievement at every opportunity.

Documenter

"As a documenter, you must keep accurate records and ensure that the project management methods meet conventional standards."

Clearly not short of an opinion, the owl steadies her tempo, concluding her oration with profound words of wisdom. "Your mission as project manager, should you choose to accept it, is essentially a call to leadership. As project manager, you may be responsible for millions of dollars in resources. Project managers must clearly understand the project outcome and the people responsible for performing the work. Project managers who understand people communicate effectively, influence what others think, and facilitate healthy conflict resolution. This requires active listening and empathizing with and acknowledging the viewpoints of others, even those with opposing points of view."

Seizing the opportunity, David sneaks in a few words between the owl's breath and her ongoing instruction to resume speaking.

"I'm wondering," he says hesitantly, "how you would define project leadership, given your initial statement of project management as a call to leadership."

Upon hearing the question, the owl appears taken aback, stunned perhaps at David's gall in interrupting her and attempting to drive the dialogue. Pausing momentarily and reflecting on the question, she turns her head slightly away, angling her neck while lowering her eyes. Her shoulders drop, and she starts to appear more approachable and supportive.

"Project leadership," she says in a lowered tone, "means knowing how and when you should establish limits and boundaries, being straightforward when communicating the message and checking in to make sure that the message is accurately received and clearly understood. Strong leadership skills mean being open to giving and receiving clear and constructive feedback that is well timed and authentic. A strong team leader must also be a team player. This means complementing the styles of others, valuing others, and empowering the team while building consensus.

"In my experience and in all of my years of managing projects and people," she continues, "I focus on building trust with my people. To me, project success requires taking the necessary action with steady, persistent effort to build a team based on trust where members are valued, understood, respected, and challenged to strive to achieve their very best. At the end of the day, project success all comes down to leadership."

"What about institutional knowledge?" David asks.

"Institutional knowledge?" the owl replies with a snicker, revealing parchment-colored teeth and a leathery smile. "You mean knowing where the dead bodies lie?"

"I guess you're right; that is what I mean," David replies humbly.

"Knowing where the dead bodies lie in an organization includes knowledge of the existing organizational structure, personnel policies, technical, interpersonal, and political factors, and failed attempts in the past. You must consider all of this when you are planning and managing a project. Information regarding the way people, teams, and organizational units behave and effective use of this information may shorten the time, cost, and effort needed to create and manage a high-performance team. As your mentor/coach I can help you out a lot with this. Feel free to leverage my expertise. I've been around for a long time, and I suppose it shows in more ways than one." She presents her offering to David tentatively and carefully, not wanting to impose.

"I willingly and gratefully take you up on that offer." David is overtly enthusiastic at the thought of leveraging the owl's expertise. "I really need to develop skills like networking, relationship building, influencing, and team leadership. I know that these skills are critical when identifying and documenting project roles and responsibilities and directing and managing the project team. I know that communication is the key," David continues.

"Efficient and effective communication plays a critical role in projects—communicating effectively; providing information in the right format, at the right time, and with the right impact and communicating efficiently; providing only the information that is needed. I've learned from firsthand experience that there is a difference between efficient and effective communication and that improper communication may delay a message delivery, relay sensitive information to the wrong audience, or prevent information from reaching some of the required stakeholders."

"I cannot thank you enough for taking time to meet with me and partnering in my development." David's gracious remarks are sincere.

"I experienced active listening, questioning, and probing ideas in our conversation today. These are life lessons. I'm certainly looking forward to our next session, and between now and then I have lots to practice." The owl and David exchange pleasantries, officially ending the mentor/ coaching session.

David's walk to the train station is slow and deliberate as he ponders what he has just learned.

Plan Your Project

David's work on the project-plan document begins. The project's complexity determines the combination of any or all of the following processes that he will complete, thereby creating a comprehensive plan:

- developing the project management plan
- categorizing and prioritizing requirements
- planning how to manage requirements
- understanding what is included in or excluded from the project
- breaking down all of the project work into work packages
- listing all activities in each work package
- sequencing all activities in each work package
- figuring out what resources are necessary to complete each activity
- determining how long it will take to complete the work of each activity
- scheduling time to complete each activity
- estimating how much it would cost to complete each scheduled activity
- determining the budget
- outlining a plan to ensure a quality product
- assigning the right people to complete each activity
- planning what, when, and how to communicate and to whom
- planning how to identify, evaluate, and address risks

- figuring out what is necessary to make or buy to pull off the project
- planning stakeholder management

The project management plan instructs key stakeholders and David, as project manager, on how the project will be executed, monitored and controlled, and closed.

As project manager, David defines, documents, and manages all work involved in the project through the project plan inclusive of all subsidiary plans. He ensures that each subsidiary management plan contains information that specifically relates to the respective knowledge area. For example, the cost management plan describes how changes to cost estimates will be reflected in the project budget and how changes or variances with a significant impact should be communicated to the project sponsor or stakeholders.

David employs active two-way communication, creating an environment where stakeholders contribute appropriately in the project-planning process from the outset. Stakeholders have skills and knowledge that must be leveraged in developing the project management plan and any subsidiary plan.

In some instances subsidiary plans are detailed. Conversely, others are simply a synopsis depending on the needs of the project. His goal is to ensure that the project plan and all subsidiary plans are integrated in a coordinated fashion.

No rule instructs him to include all subsidiary plans in every project; that would be ridiculous. Some projects are so small that including a slew of subsidiary plans is overkill.

Where the nature of the project dictates, any or all subsidiary plans listed below may be considered for inclusion in the project management plan:

- requirements management plan
- scope management plan
- schedule management plan
- cost management plan

- quality management plan
- process improvement plan
- human resources management plan
- communication management plan
- risk management plan
- procurement management plan
- stakeholder management plan

If you're into sports as David is, then the term *baseline* may be familiar to you. In baseball, the baseline is the areas within which a player must remain when running between bases. In tennis, the baseline is the back line at each end of the court. In project management, the baseline serves essentially the same purpose as it does in sports: it is the line that serves as the basis for comparison or control. It is the standard. Once David baselines the project management plan, changes may only be made via a change request generated and approved through the integrated change-control process included as a part of project execution.

Examples of project baselines include and are not limited to the following:

- schedule baseline
- cost-performance baseline
- scope baseline

Sample Template—Project Management Plan

Project Title: Automated-Sales-Management Training   **Date Prepared:** June 20XX

Project Life Cycle:

This project to design, develop, and deliver an automated-sales-management-system training will progress through phases called analysis or requirements, design, development (including testing), implementation, and evaluation. The collective phases that the project progresses through in concert are referred to as the project life cycle.

These phases are sequential and sometimes overlap. Deliverables from each phase include an analysis report, a design document, a mockup, the roll out, and the evaluation of the automated-sales-management-system training.

Variance and Baseline Management:

Schedule Variance Threshold: The critical-chain technique will be used to manage the project schedule, which includes the addition of feeder buffers and a project buffer as time reserves. A variance of one week behind schedule indicates a warning. Variances of two weeks or more are unacceptable and may result in serious schedule delays. **Cost Variance Threshold:** A variance of 5 percent over budget indicates a warning. Variances of 10 percent or more are unacceptable and may result in serious cost overruns. **Scope Variance Threshold:** The scope baseline is represented as a part of the scope statement, the work breakdown structure (WBS), and the WBS dictionary.	**Schedule, Cost, and Scope Baseline Management:** A configuration-management system with integrated change control will provide a standardized, effective, and efficient way to manage changes that relate to schedule, cost, and scope baselines. *Configuration Identification* Deliverables from each phase including an analysis report, a design document, a mockup, testing, the roll out, and the evaluation will be tracked according to schedule, cost, and scope to ensure integrity of the baseline and the corresponding deliverable. *Integrated Change Control—The Process for Reviewing and Approving Changes* The schedule, cost, and scope must be managed such that once the trigger variance is observed all proposed changes must be presented in written form and will be expected to adhere to the following procedure specified in the configuration-management and change-control system:

| Any change to the scope baseline constitutes a scope variance. No changes to the project scope are acceptable without adherence to the configuration-management and change-control process. Any unapproved change to scope may result in serious cost and/or schedule overruns with possible quality implications. | • promptly reviewing, analyzing, and approving or rejecting change requests (corrective, preventive actions, or defect repair) that may impact the schedule, cost, and scope
• managing the integrity of the project baselines and corresponding deliverables
• ensuring that the change-request processes are accompanied by information on estimated scope, time, and cost impacts
• coordinating changes across the entire project (e.g., proposed schedule changes that will often affect cost, risk, quality, and staffing)
• documenting the complete impact of the change requests.
• assuring that only approved changes are incorporated into revised baselines
• updating relevant project documents and communicating relevant information

The goal of maintaining the integrity of the schedule, cost, and scope baselines must be paramount so that only in extreme and justified circumstances should the integrated change-control process be activated at the point of crisis as opposed to the point of an early-warning trigger that may result in an acceptable as opposed to unacceptable variance. |

Project Plan Approval/Signatures

Name	Role	Signature	Date

Scope out Your Project

David has been talking to some people who told him that managing projects doesn't happen behind the desk in his cubicle. It happens on the ground, connecting with the stakeholders on and off of his register and finding out what they need or want as an outcome of the project; in other words, collecting requirements.

David understands the importance of project scoping. He's never done this before and now knows that learning doesn't always take place using the shared drive and completing online classes on the learning management system. A referral tip from the owl secures David a one-on-one tutoring session with Greg, a subject matter expert. Together, Greg and David will complete a practical walkthrough of processes including collecting requirements, creating a scope statement, creating a WBS, creating a WBS dictionary, determining logical relationships, creating a network diagram, and creating a project schedule.

"I understand from the owl that you're in the process of completing your project-planning documents related to scoping and scheduling and that you could use a little help."

"A little help is a bit of an understatement. I need a lot of help. I've been reading up on the topic and understand concepts theoretically, yet I can't produce a single document because I don't know how and where to begin," David laments.

"No worries; that's what I'm here for," Greg replies reassuringly, hoping that David is a quick study.

"Like everything else, scoping and creating a schedule is a process. It begins with categorizing and prioritizing requirements, planning how to manage requirements, understanding what is included in or excluded from the project, and breaking down all of the project work into work packages." That's the scoping aspect of it. Continuing, Greg elaborates the process for completing the project schedule.

"Creating the project schedule entails listing all activities in each work package, figuring out what resources you will need to complete each activity, determining how long it will take to complete the work of each activity, and then scheduling time to complete each activity. Any questions before I continue?"

"No questions so far."

Collecting Requirements

"Update me, David, on what you've been doing to really understand your stakeholder requirements for this project."

"I've capitalized on opportunities using multiple forums and asking stakeholders on my register to think about the outcomes that the project is intended to produce. Several of these outcomes you can touch and feel, but some of the outcomes are a service. I've asked stakeholders to describe specific conditions that these outcomes must have in place to recognize the project as a success. My goal here is to determine and prioritize the wants, needs, and expectations of all of the people and organizations that have a stake in this project."

"Is this information documented?"

"Yes." David is confident in his response. "I've written down all requirements in sufficient detail that I, or anyone else, can measure these requirements once the project work begins. I've used different techniques to get requirement information from the stakeholder: interviews, questionnaires, surveys, even observation. I stay plugged into the grapevine and the social network."

"Is there an optimum technique to use?" David asks.

"It doesn't matter which technique or combination of techniques you use to obtain stakeholder requirements," Greg responds. "The project is intended to produce the goods or services that meet their needs.

"I find it easy to group requirements into categories such as quality, performance, safety, security, technical, training, support, and maintenance, to name a few," Greg shares. "In addition to identifying, categorizing, and prioritizing requirements, I also find it useful to list the stakeholders associated with the requirements and write a couple of words that I believe capture what these stakeholders see as the mark of acceptance. I find it makes good sense to think this process through early on in the planning. You may come to see later that having this information is a great tool when making trade-off decisions among requirements and in managing stakeholder expectations."

"Thanks for the tip." David makes copious notes.

"It's important to have a plan to manage requirements throughout your project," Greg continues. "This is another one of those plans that you can't just make up, keep in your head, and not tell anybody about. Just because you have to write down a plan doesn't mean that you have to come up with something fancy. Something simple will do. Make sure that you include the following:

- technique you plan to use to collect the requirements
- categories that will be used to group the requirements
- approach that you will use to prioritize the requirements
- attributes that you will use to trace the requirements
- procedure needed to change the requirements
- process for determining the impact of the change
- different methods that will be used to verify the requirements

"The time taken to collect your requirements is time well spent. This is where scoping begins. Collecting requirements is the process of uncovering everything that stakeholders want." Greg pauses for a while as David catches up with his note taking. "Take a look at this example of stakeholder requirements for a basic training program."

Example—Basic Training Stakeholder Requirements

- formalized learning program
- measurable outcomes to job-performance standards
- program tailored to performance needs of both male and female employees
- learning program divided into courses
- courses divided into lessons
- lessons supported by written lesson plans
- lesson plans include the following information:

- o learning objectives
- o materials/supplies needed
- o time needed
- o procedures as it relates to how lesson will be introduced
- o instructional strategy/learning activities
- o individual/group classroom or online activity and instructions for debrief
- o performance measures and evaluation
- sign of approval from the department head

"This simple example presents everything that the stakeholders want in the project as it relates to deliverable," Greg continues.

Defining Scope

"If collecting requirements uncovers everything that stakeholders want, then defining scope determines what stakeholders will actually get as deliverables."

"Oh!" exclaims David, "is that want they mean by in and out of scope?"

"Yes. In defining scope, you should develop a common understanding of what is included in or excluded from your project. Scope is collectively the product, service, or result of the project.

"Tell me, David, what is the difference between product and project scope?"

"My understanding is that product scope refers to the product, the features and characteristics that describe the product, service, or result of the project. Project scope describes the project management work. The process of defining the product or project scope begins with a review of the project objectives. Objectives describe what you are trying to accomplish or produce as a result of the project. Objectives should be quantifiable and may include schedule, cost, quality, or business measures."

"Accurate definition. Where do you get this information from?"

"Can I get this information from any documents or information that I can get my hands on that outline the project requirements or any other standard policies or guidelines?"

"Yes, you can. I also use that approach. Additionally, over the years I've found the use of several tools and techniques that define the project scope to be very useful. In looking at ways to convert the product description and project objectives into tangible outcomes I often explore several alternatives. Brainstorming with others and thinking outside of the box are ways that I use to explore alternatives to accomplishing the project work. These techniques may also prove beneficial to you, David.

"At the end of the day, the scope definition process results in the creation of the scope statement."

"Aaah, yes," David chimes in. "I've read about the purpose and use of the scope statement to document the project objectives, tangible outcomes, and work required to produce these tangible outcomes. I understand that this is a key document that may be used to direct the project team's work and serve as a basis for future decisions."

"I'm telling you, David, the project scope statement is one of my 'must have' documents. I never manage a project without having this document by my side."

"Really?"

"Really. David, the project scope statement serves as an agreement between the project and the customer. This agreement states precisely what the work of the project will produce. This document serves as a baseline for the project and tells everyone concerned with the project exactly what they will get when the project work is complete."

"Wow! I'm happy that we're having this conversation. I was contemplating not writing a scope statement in the interest of time."

"David, the scope statement includes the product scope description, the product acceptance criteria, and project outcomes, exclusions, constraints, and assumptions."

"Wait a minute, Greg—what do you mean by exclusions?"

"Exclusion is anything that is not included as a deliverable or work of the project. Be sure to note project exclusions in the project scope statement so that they may be used to manage stakeholder expectations throughout the project. Constraints are anything that either restricts the actions of the project team or dictates the actions of the project team."

"Would time, budget, scope, quality, resources, and so on be considered as constraints?"

"Yes, and don't forget assumptions. Assumptions for the purpose of project management are concepts that you believe to be true. Identifying, documenting, and updating assumptions in project management is undertaken so that they may be validated and so that contingency plans may be created. Information to add to the list of assumptions may be sourced from stakeholders and brainstorming exercises with the project team as well as from vendors or suppliers." Greg relieves his parched throat with a long drink of cold water.

Example—Basic Training Scope Statement

Product Scope Description

Design, develop, and deliver a formal learning program for male and female employees that closes knowledge and skill gaps required to meet performance standards and/or objectives on the job.

Project Deliverables

• formal learning program for all employees • lesson plans • classroom session • self-study completion • handouts to employees for completion as a self-study activity • completion and sign-off of self-study assignments completed by employees • practical use of the system

Acceptance Criteria

• a plan that outlines the structure of the formal learning program • learning content that is easy to understand and relevant • weekly status reports to ensure that requirements are adhered to • support materials

- a change-control process to facilitate required changes
- learning objectives and performance outcomes linked to job performance
- method/systems of measurement
- sign-off by stakeholders
- sustainability

Exclusions

- service officers
- senior-management-level officers
- back-office employees

Constraints

- fixed budget
- fixed delivery date
- limited resources
- necessary training that may conflict with other initiatives and may shift the focus elsewhere
- logistical constraints

Assumptions

- endorsement of initiative from the sponsor
- supplies/equipment and/or resources provided
- budget covering the cost of requirements
- buy-in from key stakeholders
- access to training facilities
- sponsor who remains committed and consistently demonstrates a high level of enthusiasm toward the project from the beginning to the end
- project not undermined
- no bottlenecks when decisions need to be made quickly
- approvals not cumbersome and lengthy

Version History		
Version	Date	Comments

Creating the Work-Breakdown Structure

"The next step is to create the work-breakdown structure, or WBS," Greg continues. "Are you familiar with the WBS, David?"

"I've heard about it, but I really don't know that much about it."

"Okay, I'll explain. The WBS clearly describes the project's deliverables and scope. The WBS defines and organizes the project work."

"How does this help me as project manager?" questions David.

"Well, it assists you as project manager as well the project team and stakeholders in developing a clear vision of the project's end products or outcomes.

"Do you now understand how this document assists you as a project manager?"

"Not really. Maybe as you continue to explain it will become clearer to me."

"Very well then; I'll go on. The WBS divides the project scope into manageable packages of work, which also provides support for focusing communication with stakeholders. It assists you in clearly identifying accountability to a level of detail necessary for effectively managing and controlling the project."

"Oh, I see where you are going now. The WBS facilitates the reporting and analyzing of project and status data, including resource allocations, cost estimates, expenditures, and performance." David beams as the light bulb goes off in this head.

"You got it, David." Greg's excitement is evident in his voice.

"The information from the project scope statement and the requirement documentation as well as standard policies, guidelines, templates, and other requirements is essential when creating the WBS. The WBS dictionary supports the WBS with an explanation of what is included as a part of the respective work package."

100-Percent Rule

"As I mentioned before," Greg continues, "the WBS includes 100 percent of the work defined by the project scope. Collectively, all levels of the WBS roll up to the top so that all project work is captured and no additional work is added."

"What happens if someone asks you to complete an activity that is not included as a part of the WBS?" David asks tentatively.

"That's an issue." Greg retorts. "The WBS should not include any work that falls outside the actual scope of the project—that is, the WBS cannot include more than 100 percent of the work. The 100-percent rule also applies at the activity level. The work represented by the activities in each work package must add up to 100 percent of the work necessary to complete the work package.

"I've presented for you the five steps that I use to create a WBS. They're written out for you. That saves you some ink, David," Greg says sarcastically.

"Thanks, man."

"I've also brought along a basic WBS to work-package level and a sample WBS dictionary submission. Take a look at these documents." Greg pauses, giving David time to review and digest the material.

Basic Training—Steps in Creating a WBS

1. Identify the deliverables.
2. Organize the project work and determine the WBS structure.
3. Break down the WBS components into lower-level components.
4. Assign identification codes.
5. Verify the WBS by examining the breakdown and determine whether all components are clear and complete.

Basic Training—WBS to Work-Package Level

1.0 Formal learning program for male and female employees
1.1 Prepping
1.2 Classroom
1.3 Self-study

Sample WBS Dictionary

Project Title: Automated-Sales-Management Training   **Date Prepared:** June 20XX

Work Package Name: Initiating	WBS ID: 1.1.2 Control Account Number: ISD-112-02

Description of Work: The purpose of initiating a project is to authorize the project, produce a high-level definition of the project, and identify the stakeholders. The typical outputs of initiating a project include the project charter, and the stakeholder register. This work package includes activities that should be completed as a part of initiating a project.

Milestones:
1. Initiating documents (project charter, stakeholder register)

Due Dates:
June 14, 20XX

ID	Activity	Resource	Labor			Material			Total Cost
			Hours	Rate	Total	Units	Overhead Cost	Total	
1.1.2.1	Initiating documents	Jane Doe	10 hrs	$10	$100	NA	NA	NA	$100

Quality Requirements:
Use knowledge and skill in project management as the basis for creating project-initiating documents that are consistent with requirements outlined in the standard organizational procedures. Establish clear linkages that are traceable from one initiating document to the next as it relates to content presented in corresponding fields, such as requirements and identifying initial risks.

Acceptance Criteria:
The requirement used to accept the WBS element is strict adherence to conventional project management practices as outlined in the organizational procedures. This acceptance criterion is outlined as a part of the quality-success criteria in the project charter, requirements documentation, and scope statement.

Technical Information:
The technical information as it relates to this WBS element is found in the latest edition of the organizational procedures and guidelines handbook.

Contract Information:
No contractual relationship is applicable. This WBS element is performed by a salaried employee of the organization.

Scheduling

Defining Activities

"Proceed or take a break?"

"Let's continue, Greg. I can always take a break later, but I really need this information now."

"Very well; we'll continue. With knowledge of the project's intended deliverables in hand, your next step is to successfully organize and manage your time to achieve desired outcomes. Be sure to support each element of the project scope with an activity or activities that will result in completion of the work. Defining activities documents the specific activities needed to fulfill the requirements detailed in the project scope."

"Why can't you just list the activities?" David asks, trying to not sound as if his intent is to bail out of doing more work.

"You are listing the activities, but without describing associated work it could be open to multiple interpretations, don't you think?"

"I see your point, Greg."

"Each activity describes the work that must be accomplished. The description of each activity must begin with a verb and contain a unique object. When you write these descriptions for each activity, David, write them in a way that describes a specific piece of work. A single person should be responsible for performing the activity. This is not to say that multiple resources may not be required to accomplish the activity, but it does require that a single person is responsible for the performance. Take a look at the example that I brought as an illustration of what I am explaining."

Basic Training—Activity List

Project Title: Basic Training   **Date Prepared:** July 20XX

ID	Activity	Description of Work
1.1.1	Write lesson plans.	This document outlines the purpose, learning objectives, materials/supplies, time, procedures, instructions of activity, and debrief as well as performance

		measures and evaluation for each lesson included as a part of the basic training program.
1.2.1	Introduce lesson.	Sets the context for the respective lesson, including purpose, learning objectives, and performance outcomes, establishing ground rules, creating and obtaining expectations, and establishing structure.
1.2.1.1	Ask questions.	Facilitate discussion questions orally in a large or small group format with facilitator-assisted exchange.
1.3.1	Issue handouts to males.	Provide male employees with handouts inclusive of instructions for proper completion, assessment, measurement, and sustainment.
1.3.1.1	Issue handouts to females.	Provide female employees with handouts inclusive of instructions for proper completion, assessment, measurement, and support.
1.3.2	Work on handouts for males.	Initiate completion of problem-solving activities/exercises (small group and whole group) for male employees.
1.3.2.1	Work on handouts for females.	Initiate completion of problem-solving activities/exercises (small group and whole group) for female employees.
1.4.1	Issue sign-off instructions.	Facilitator issues performance measures based on performance-outcome requirements that are determined by the employee's demonstrated application of required activities and/or exercises as stated performance outcomes in the context of their gender groups.
1.4.1.1	Complete assignment for males.	Complete all requirements communicated by facilitator in accordance with requisite performance standards for gender group.
1.4.1.2	Complete assignment for females.	Complete all requirements communicated by facilitator in accordance with requisite performance standards for gender group.

Sequencing Activities

"Are you with me, David?"

"Yes, Greg. I'm tracking with you."

"Good. Once you define the list of activities, you must determine and record the order in which the activities will be performed. The first step to sequencing activities in logical order is to find out whether dependencies exist among the activities. The precedence-diagramming method (PDM) is a technique used for constructing a schedule model in which activities are linked by one or more logical relationships to show the sequences that are to be performed."

"I've got to stop you—I need clarification on the PDM."

"The PDM," Greg explains, "includes four types of dependencies or logical relationships. A predecessor activity is an activity that comes before a dependent activity in a schedule. A successor activity is a dependent activity that logically comes after another activity on a schedule. You must sequence logical relationships between activities correctly if you want to develop a realistic and achievable schedule. To avoid creating artificial or incorrect activity relationships, initial activity sequencing should be determined independent of resource availability. There are four types of logical relationships:

1. Finish-to-start (FS)
2. Start-to-finish (SF)
3. Finish-to-finish (FF)
4. Start-to-start (SS)

Write down these simple, everyday examples that I use to illustrate the four types of logical relationships."

Finish-to-Start Relationship

"A finish-to-start relationship is a logical relationship in which a successor activity cannot start until a predecessor activity is finished. For example, when you have finished writing the project charter, present it to the sponsor for sign-off; you cannot obtain sign-off on the charter until after you have finished writing it.

Start-to-Finish Relationship

"A start-to-finish relationship is a logical relationship in which a successor activity cannot finish until a predecessor activity has started. For example, the applause cannot finish until the speaker starts talking.

Finish-to-Finish Relationship

"A finish-to-finish relationship is a logical relationship in which a successor activity cannot finish until a predecessor activity is finished. An example of this is cooking steak and potatoes on the barbecue. This relationship is based on ending times. Both activities can start whenever they need to as long as they finish at the same time.

Start-to-Start Relationship

"A start-to-start relationship is a logical relationship in which a successor activity cannot start until a predecessor activity has started. For example, as soon as the bride starts walking down the aisle, start taking the pictures. This relationship is based on activity start times. The ending times of each activity are not related; one activity can end at a much later time than the other.

Estimating Activity Resources and Duration

"What do you understand about sequencing activities, David?"

"I understand that just because activities are associated according to a work package in some order, this does not necessarily mean that they are networked in the same order to complete the project work. This is where PDM comes in. When activities are sequenced using the PDM scheduling model, they are associated based on their dependencies or logical relationship. This supports the proper completion of the project work."

"Good recap."

"All projects from the smallest to the largest require resources."

"When you say resources, do you mean people?"

"The physical resources needed to complete a project include people, equipment, supplies, and materials. Estimating activity resources is concerned with determining the types and quantities of human and material resources needed for each scheduled activity. Estimating activity resources should be closely coordinated with estimating costs, as resources are typically the largest expense that you will have on any project."

"Are you clear with the explanation of estimating activity resources before I continue by explaining estimating activity duration?"

"I'm clear; continue."

"When you estimate activity duration, you are looking at the work effort, resources, and number of work periods needed to complete each activity. Estimating activity durations uses information on the activity scope of work, required resource types, estimated resource quantities, and resource calendars. Activity-duration estimates are quantifiable estimates expressed as the number of work periods needed to complete a scheduled activity."

"When you say work period what are you referring to hours or days?"

"Yes, and on large projects duration estimates may be expressed in weeks or months. Activity-duration estimates are expressed in work periods, and the estimates become inputs to developing the schedule. When you are estimating activity duration, make certain to include all the time that will elapse from the beginning of the activity until the work is completed."

"How am I supposed to know all the time that will elapse from the beginning of the activity until the work is completed?"

"For this information, David, rely on people who are most knowledgeable of the activities you are trying to estimate. They will help with this process. Take a look at the activity-duration estimates for the basic training project that we are discussing as an illustration of these concepts."

Basic Training—Activity-Duration Estimates

Project Title: Basic Training   **Date Prepared:** July 20XX

WBS ID	Activity	Effort Hours	Duration Estimate
1.1.1	Write lesson plans.	35 hours	5 days
1.2.1	Introduce lesson.	7 hours	1 day
1.2.1.1	Ask questions.	14 hours	2 days
1.3.1	Issue handouts to males.	7 hours	1 day
1.3.1.1	Issue handouts to females.	21 hours	3 days
1.3.2	Work on handouts for males.	35 hours	5 days
1.3.2.1	Work on handouts for females.	105 hours	15 days
1.4.1	Issue sign-off instructions.	14 hours	2 days
1.4.1.1	Complete assignment for males.	84 hours	12 days
1.4.1.2	Complete assignment for females.	126 hours	18 days

Developing a Schedule

"We are now onto developing a schedule. David, I have to leave in fifteen minutes for another meeting, although I'm sure we will be done before then. The schedule-network-analysis technique relies on sequential networks where one activity occurs before the next, or a series of activities occur concurrently before the next series of activities begin, and so on, on a single duration estimate for each activity. Although we have completed these tasks already, write down these three requirements to produce a network diagram for future reference. Then take a look at the network diagram showing activity sequence for basic training that I'll explain to you in detail."

Requirements to Produce a Network Diagram

1. Create a list of activities to complete for the project.
2. Sequence the activities in the order in which they must occur; determine predecessor and successor.
3. Estimate the time required to complete each activity.

Precedence-Diagramming Method (PDM)
Showing Activity Sequence for Basic Training

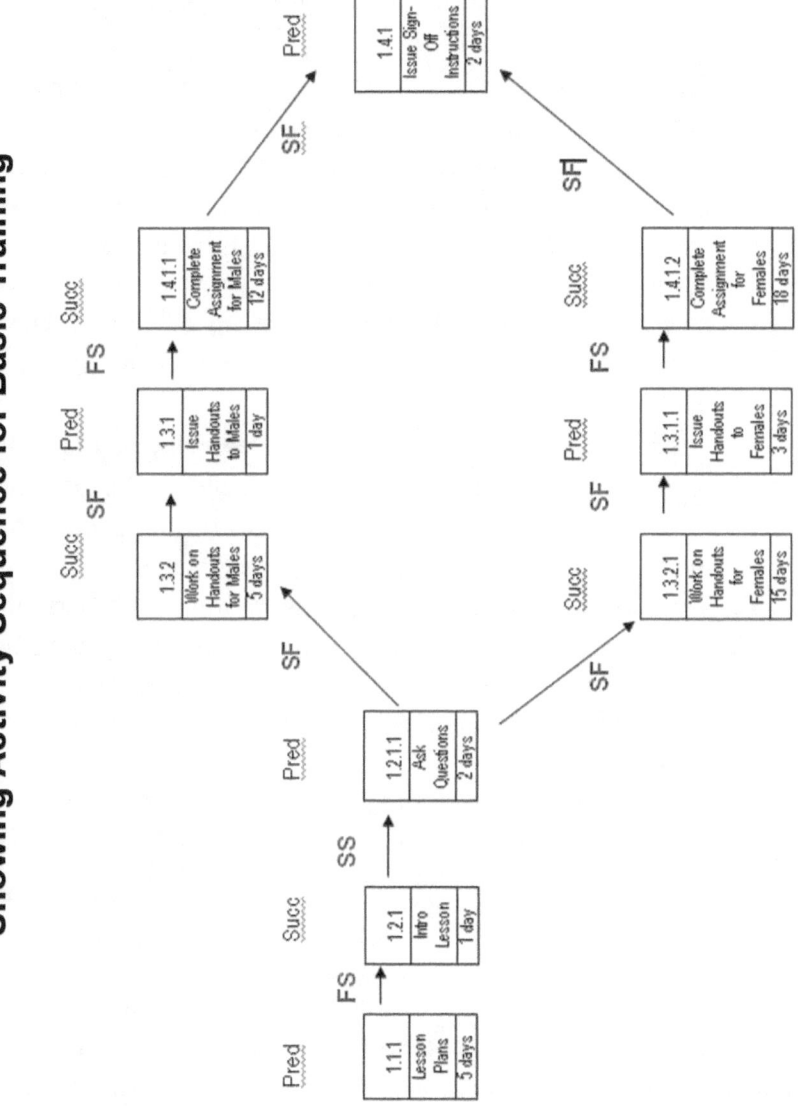

Basic Training—Interpretation of Network Diagram

"David, I typed up the explanation of the network diagram so that you don't have to takes notes and instead you can be focused on understanding the logic. The network diagram begins as follows:

- The instructor takes five days to finish writing lesson plans before starting to introduce the lesson.
- The instructor starts introducing the lesson by asking questions. Given the length of the lesson, both activities finish at different times, but the predecessor cannot start until the successor starts.
- It takes two days for the instructor to ask questions. The male and female employees cannot finish working on handouts until the instructor starts asking questions.
- The males and females can only start working on the handouts after the instructor issues them. It takes one day for the instructor to issue the handouts to the males and three days for the instructor to issue the handouts to the females.
- The handouts must be issued before the males and females can complete their respective assignments. It takes twelve days for the males to complete their assignments, and it takes eighteen days for the females to complete their assignment.
- As soon as the male and female employees finish completing assignments the instructor starts issuing sign-off instructions. It takes two days for the instructor to issue sign-off instructions.

"After confirmation and agreement that my network diagram is logical and that all activities are represented, I input the information into a scheduling software tool to produce a schedule. A project schedule is the result of defining activities, sequencing activities, estimating activity resources, and estimating activity duration and is used to assist you with managing time on your project."

"David, I'm very proud of you. I was hopeful that you would be a quick study based on the positive words that the owl told me on your behalf, and you have certainly lived up to expectations. I'm rushing off to my next meeting and only have five minutes to get there; send me a meeting invite if you want to talk."

With that, Greg is gone.

Let's Talk Money

Show me the money, put your money where your mouth is, money talks—these are all common ways that we use to express the fact that nine times out of ten, we will get to the point where we have to talk money. You know, the thing that makes the world go round or the root of all evil, depending on the way you see things.

David knows that on a project, just as in any other aspect of life where securing capital is required, it is necessary to develop cost estimates for all resources for each scheduled activity. As Greg explained, resources include labor, materials, equipment, services, facilities, inflation allowance, and contingency costs, and each of these has a corresponding cost. The process of estimating costs includes weighing alternative options and examining risks and trade-offs.

After looking at the budget, David considers some alternatives, such as make versus buy, buy versus lease, and sharing resources either across projects or departments. He realizes that he must include all costs associated with the project over its entire life cycle as a part of his cost estimates.

Cost estimates are usually expressed in units of some currency (e.g., dollars). Other units of measure, such as days or staff hours, may be used to facilitate comparisons, eliminating the effects of currency fluctuations.

Information from a host of areas may be used when estimating costs. David realizes that project documents like the scope statement, the work-breakdown structure, and the work-breakdown structure dictionary that he took hours to compile will come in handy right about now. Information on key deliverables, constraints, and assumptions may be necessary when estimating costs.

David uses information from the project schedule, such as the type and quantity of resources and the amount of time that those resources are applied. These are major factors in determining costs. He'll also need to look in the external environment in which his project operates to discover additional factors such as market conditions and regional or global supply-and-demand conditions that may influence cost. He recognizes that there are many approaches that he may consider to obtain the information that he needs to estimate cost.

"I'd better schedule some appointments with subject matter experts to get valuable information on costs that relate to labor rates, material costs, inflation, risk factors, and other variables," he thinks aloud.

Experts may often provide valuable insights about the environment and information from prior similar projects. If he can't speak with an expert, what are alternative ways to gather this information? Perhaps he can review records from previous projects that are similar in scope, cost, budget, and duration to the one that he is presently working on.

He also needs to think about a contingency allowance (referred to as reserve analysis) a technique that may be used to account for cost uncertainty. Perhaps David may use a percentage of the estimated cost as a contingency reserve. As more precise information about his project becomes available, he may use the contingency reserve, or he may reduce or eliminate it completely. He must remember to clearly identify the contingency reserve in the cost determination.

The next step is to determine the budget, add activity-cost estimates, and establish a cost-performance baseline to be used as a measurement tool for the project. Only the costs associated with the project become part of the authorized project budget, which will be used as a plan for allocating costs to project activities.

Project Budget Form

Activity Code	Project Task	Labor Hours	Labor Costs $	Material Cost $	Travel Cost $	Other Costs $	Total Cost per Task

Project Cumulative Cost Chart

Month of Project	Projected Monthly Cost	Projected Cumulative Cost	Actual Monthly Cost	Actual Cumulative Cost

Don't Forget Quality

Sometime later in a stakeholder meeting David poses this scenario: "You're involved in a situation. You expect a certain outcome. Your mind is geared up; your excitement and anticipation level at an all-time high. But when the moment of truth arrives, what you expect to get is so far removed from what you actually get that you can't believe your eyes." Nodding heads is a popular response from the group.

"If you relate to this experience," David proceeds, "then you understand fundamentally the importance of quality."

David goes on to describe the definition of quality as meeting stakeholders' expectations. The process of planning quality should focus on targeting quality standards relevant to the project at hand. As a goal, devise a plan to meet and satisfy those standards.

When questioned on the significance of the quality management plan, David responds, "The quality management plan describes how the project management team will implement the quality policy during the course of the project."

Another question is posed from the group: "What about the process improvement plan as a key output of the quality planning process?"

In response, David describes the process improvement plan as documenting the actions for analyzing processes to increase customer satisfaction.

Identifying quality requirements or standards for projects and products must be done when planning quality. This includes documenting how projects will demonstrate compliance. Quality planning should take place in conjunction with other planning processes. For example, proposed changes in the product to meet identified quality standards may require cost or schedule adjustments and a detailed risk analysis.

Remember those project documents that David took hours compiling? Great news again—his labor is not in vain. Behold the power of recycling. He will use information in these documents in many ways again and again for different reasons. This is why it is very important that project documents are not only completed but are completed correctly.

Recall that the scope statement contains the project description, major project deliverables, and acceptance criteria. David is well advised to review the product scope description, as it will often contain details of technical issues and other concerns that may affect quality planning. The definition of acceptance criteria may impact project costs and quality costs.

He should also consider reviewing the stakeholder register when planning quality, as it identifies stakeholders with a particular interest in or impact on quality. The risk register is another document that David may review when planning quality. This document includes information on threats and opportunities that may impact quality requirements.

Always consider the environment in any conversation about quality, David recalls from a previous coaching session with the owl.

"I look at government agency regulations, rules, standards, and guidelines specific to the application area as well as the working or operating conditions of the project or product," the owl had advised. "All of these considerations may affect project quality."

There are many approaches that David considers to obtain the information needed to plan quality. He considers a cost-benefit analysis that compares the cost to produce the product, service, or result of the project to the benefit that the organization will receive as a result of executing the project. Cost-benefit analysis includes the costs to produce the product or service, the costs to take the product to market, and the ongoing operational support costs.

He also considers the trade-offs of the cost of quality. It is cheaper and more efficient to prevent defects in the first place than to spend time and money fixing them later.

In preparing activity-cost estimates, he may have made some assumptions about the cost of quality, which is the total cost to produce the product or service of the project according to the quality standards. This cost includes all the work necessary to meet the product requirements, whether the work is planned or unplanned. It also includes the cost of work performed due to nonconformance to quality requirements, assessing whether the project or service meets requirements, and rework.

Concluding the stakeholder meeting with questions and answers is usual and customary. Requests are made for clarification on prevention costs, appraisal costs, and failure costs, defined as the three costs associated with quality. David recaps: "Prevention costs are associated with satisfying customer requirements by producing a product without defects. These costs are manifested early in the process and include aspects such as training, design review, internal and external review, sign-off cycles, and contractor and supplier costs. Appraisal costs are incurred to examine the product or process, making certain that requirements are met. Appraisal costs might include costs associated with aspects such as inspections and testing. Failure costs are incurred when things do not go according to plan. They are also known as the cost of poor quality. Internal failure costs result when customer requirements are not satisfied while the product is still in your control. Internal failure costs may include corrective action, rework, scrapping, and downtime. External failure costs occur when the product has reached the customer and the customer determines that the requirements are not met. Costs associated with external failure costs might include inspections at the customer site, returns, and customer service costs.

The quality management plan describes how the project manager and the project team will carry out the quality policy and documents the resources needed to carry out the quality plan. The quality management plan outlines all processes and procedures that should be used to satisfy quality requirements, including quality control, quality assurance techniques, and continuous improvement processes." As project manager, David writes the quality management plan along with the project team. Quality actions may be assigned to the work packages on the work-breakdown structure based on the quality plan requirements.

The quality management plan describes how the quality policy will be implemented. This document describes quality control and quality assurance procedures. Outlined below is a sample of a quality management plan for the automated-sales-management training project.

Quality Management Plan

Project Name:	Automated-Sales-Management-Training Project
Prepared By:	You
Date:	Yesterday

1. Department's Quality Policy—ADDIE Model			

Analysis	Design	Develop and Implement	Evaluate
Conduct needs and performance analysis according to department standards.	Use department design document template. Create SMART learning objectives and performance outcomes that are directly linked to learning content.	Use department standard format template.	Analyze evaluation forms and reports based on department evaluation standards.
Select tasks/ functions for sales officers.	Sequence the learning and/ or performance objectives.	Select content-presentation strategy.	Use standardized evaluation form.
Construct performance measures.	Insert activities (one-third presentation; two-thirds application) and feedback activities, test, and performance measures.	Present content in standard format template.	Performance checklist to measure performance on the job.
Conduct internal review and sign-off on job analysis.	Conduct internal review and sign-off on design document.	Conduct internal review and sign-off on learner and facilitator guide.	

2. Project Quality Definition

Quality in project execution is defined as follows:
- Stakeholder's expectations are met.
- Every aspect of the ADDIE model is built into the instructional design of the learning solution.
- There is strict adherence to the quality standards as it relates to style guide.
- Minimal grammar/spelling mistakes are evident upon first review.
- All grammar/spelling mistakes are corrected and not evident in final learner and facilitator guides.

3. Deliverables and Acceptable Criteria

Deliverables	Acceptance Criteria/Applicable Standards
1. Job analysis	Adherence to ADDIE model
2. Design document	Adherence to ADDIE model and organization's standard design document template
3. Project management plan	Adherence to project management methodology outlined in the *PMBOK Guide* most recent edition
4. Learner and facilitator guides	• Clear, concise instructions for the learner and facilitator • No spelling/grammar mistakes • Adherence to ADDIE model
5. Project management plan (updates)	Adherence to project management methodology outlined in the *PMBOK Guide* most recent edition
6. Creation and analysis of Level 1 and Level 3 evaluations	Adherence to ADDIE model
7. Project-closing documents	Adherence to project management methodology outlined in the *PMBOK Guide* most recent edition

4. Quality Check Activities

Quality assurance activities for the project will include the items listed below:
- internal review with corresponding sign-off prior to onward transmission to stakeholders for design document
- first and second internal review with corresponding sign-off on learner and facilitator guide prior to production
- clear and well-written publishing instructions
- lessons-learned and feedback discussions at the end of each project phase to ensure that requirements are correct, complete, and accurately reflect stakeholder needs

5. Project Monitoring and Control

- Updates to the project management plan will monitor and control variances from respective baselines.
- Delays or impacts to budget are proactively reported to the department manager along with recommended solution through weekly status reports.

Getting Good People

Between bites of her sandwich during a regular coaching session, the owl challenges David: "Think about the activities that must be completed on your project." She pauses to avoid choking on lunch. "Think about the human resources needed to complete those activities. What document would you use to determine your human resources needs?"

The owl continues: "As project manager, you may develop a human resources plan documenting the roles and responsibilities of individuals or groups performing activities as well as the reporting relationships between them."

Continuing, she informs David of the things that go into developing the human resources plan for any project. These include the following:

- identifying project roles and responsibilities
- documenting project roles
- defining the skills needed for the project
- stating the responsibilities and required skills
- identifying reporting relationships
- creating the staffing management plan

"Consider the availability of resources, skill levels, and training needs when developing your human resources plan," the owl admonishes. "These factors impact project cost, schedule, and quality and may produce risks not previously considered. You may ask the following questions when acquiring staff:

- Will the human resources come from within the organization or externally?
- Will team members need to work in a central location, or can they work from distant locations?
- What are the costs associated with each level of expertise needed for the project?

- How much assistance can the organization's human resources department and functional managers provide to the project management team?

"One of your goals is to produce a staffing management plan as a part of the process of developing the human resources plan. The staffing management plan describes when and how human resources requirements will be met."

Concluding lunch and the coaching session with these words of wisdom, she states, "Be sure to continually update your staffing management plan during the project. This plan is used to direct the process of acquiring and developing team members. Information that you should consider include acquiring staff, a resource calendar to indicate when resources are available, a staff release plan, training needs, recognition and rewards, and compliance and safety."

Sample Human Resources Plan

Project Title: JJ Enterprises Records Management

Date Prepared: June 20XX

Roles, Responsibilities, and Authority:

Role:	Authority:	Responsibility:
1. Project Manager	1. Accept ultimate responsibility for completion, acceptance, and status reporting for all project deliverables	1. Needs analysis, initiating, design, project planning, developing and implementing, executing and monitoring, evaluating, training, and closing
2. Programmer	2. Complete all assignments related to the automated records components of the records management system including not limited to programming	2. Hardware, platform, data conversion, custom modules, and programming respective components in keeping with all instructions provided by the procurement statement of work

Project Organizational Structure

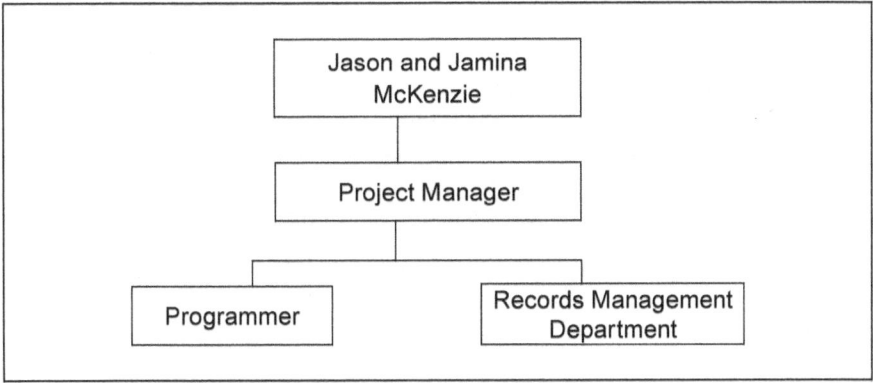

Staffing Management Plan

Staff Acquisition:

External Environmental Factors
- Project manager will be identified based on project requirements.
- Programmer will be identified based on prior experience and data obtained from external environmental factors as it relates to records management projects of requisite scope.
- Resource availability will be confirmed for the dates and period in question.
- Resources will be preassigned to the project and identified as such in requisite project-planning documents.
- Negotiations will begin immediately after project-initiating documents are signed to secure respective vendor.
- Approval will be sought from respective vendor and JJ Enterprises staff members to access their expertise during project planning to ensure accuracy of project documents.

Onboarding Procedures
- Onboarding procedures will adhere to standard conventions as it relates to organizational policies at JJ Enterprises.
- Contracts with respective vendor will be signed to secure professional services from programmers during the period in question.
- All project team members will be invited to the project kickoff for a formal introduction to each other as well as to the project.
- Project team members will be included in team brainstorming and team-building initiatives in keeping with what is outlined in the project communication plan.

Staff Release:

- Procedures for releasing staff will adhere to standard conventions in JJ Enterprises. Such policies and procedures include and are not limited to conventions for completing requisite project templates, knowledge transfer, capturing project historical data, and storage of project information on the project management information system.
- All project team members will be invited to project close-out celebrations as well as included in focus groups to capture lessons-learned information.

Resource Calendars:

Resources calendars will describe the time frames in which the resources will be needed on the project and when the recruitment process should begin. Resources may be described individually, by teams, or by functions (i.e., programmers, testers, and so on).

Training Needs:

Training that relates to company processes will include job-aid format and job shadowing. Such training is necessary to ensure adherence to communication and general office practices and protocol used in JJ Enterprise projects.

Rewards and Recognition:

Rewards and recognition processes will include the following:
- Points may be awarded by staff for tasks/deliverables that meet or exceed quality, time, and cost requirements.
- Points may be redeemable for gifts based on the dollar value of the respective gift.
- Points and gift awards will be celebrated during weekly pump-up meetings.
- Team achievements will also be celebrated in a newsletter that will be created to facilitate communication and information sharing on the project.
- Rewards and recognition will also be included as a part of the project close-out celebration.

Regulations, Standards, and Policy Compliance:

- The conventional records management practices and procedures related to industry standards are included.
- Technical standards are included as a part of the automated records component as it relates to computer hardware, platform, data conversion, and custom modules.

Safety:

Safety regulations, equipment, training, or procedures as it relates to the roles, authority, and responsibility are outlined in JJ Enterprise guideline for behavior on the company premises.

Automated-Sales-Training
Responsible Accountable Consult Inform Matrix (RACI)

	Core Project Team		Extended Team	
	Project Manager	Vendor	Reviewers	Subject Matter Experts
Needs Analysis				
1.1.1.1 Analysis Report	A		C	C
Initiating				
1.1.2.1 Initiating Docs	A		S	C
Design				
1.1.3.1 Design Doc	A		S	C
Project Planning				
1.1.4.1 Planning Docs	A		S	C
Develop & Implement				
1.1.5.1 Analyze System	A	R	C	C
1.1.5.2 Assess System Capability	A	R	C	C
1.1.5.3 Make Recommendations	A	R	C	C
Execute & Monitor				
1.1.6.1 Executing & Monitor Docs	A		C	I
Evaluating				
1.1.7.1 Conducting Evaluation	A		C	C
Training				
1.1.8.1 Key Stakeholders	A		C	C
Closing				
1.1.9.1 Close Project	A		C	C

Legend:

A Accountable = Ultimate responsibility for completion, acceptance, and status reporting for project deliverable

R Responsible = Actually performing activities in completing a project deliverable

C Consulted = Must review and provide input into the completion of a project deliverable

I Informed = Informed of status of completion of project deliverable

S Sign Off = Authority to sign off a project deliverable

Effective Communication Is Key

Before checking his messages and completing a few tasks, David changes his clothes after participating as a company representative in the annual five-kilometer fun run in support of environmental clean-up efforts. He has consumed enough energy drink to last a lifetime.

"Wow!" exclaims David's colleague as he races through the door. "Where's the first-place geriatric-division-winning trophy?"

"If you don't mind, any messages?"

"From the boss. He wants you to return his call."

David decides to return the call to the boss before powering up his computer to check e-mails and plug himself into all tracking and monitoring electronic devices.

"Did he say what he wanted?" he asks, taking a bit of paper from his colleague's hand on which he had scrawled the words *communication plan.*

"He wouldn't say, just that it is important."

Feeling his adrenaline level rising, David punches in the boss's telephone number and wonders if it is good news or bad.

"This is David. I heard that you called for me?" he asks with no exchange of pleasantries.

"Looks like we're slipping on some deliverable dates; I expected the communication plan some time ago," the boss says. "Listen, skip the communication plan. There's no time for it. Besides, it's not that important anyway."

"Cut a communication plan? Now that's a novel idea." David shakes his head, sinking into his chair. "What's next?"

"Just meet my deadlines. I've pulled a few strings, and I was able to get a short extension for the plan on my desk tomorrow afternoon. I'm afraid that's the best that I can do."

"Boss, I need you to trust me on this—we can't shave out the communication plan. Can we cut a deal? If I have a project plan on your desk tomorrow afternoon including the communication plan, could that work?"

"What's the big deal with the communication plan, David? Save yourself some sleep—I'm okay without it!"

"It certainly may reduce the likelihood of the project being derailed." David swallows hard, holding his breath.

"Whatever you can do isn't enough, David. Do about twice that much. Just have the project plan on my desk tomorrow afternoon."

"Thanks, boss. I know I will."

"Did you hear that?" David questions his colleague.

"A bit. It sounded pretty intense. What's the deal with the communication plan? Why do it, man? Save yourself the headache. What goes into it anyway?"

"The communication needs of the stakeholders, the types of information necessary, the format for communicating the information, how often the information is distributed, and who prepares it—that's just the beginning.

"The communication plan should document the approach that will be taken to ensure efficient and effective communication with your stakeholders. Effective communication means that information is provided in the right format, at the right time, and with the right impact. Efficient communication means that you provide only the information that is needed. Your communication plan may represent communication across several dimensions. Examples are internal (within the project), external (with the customer, other projects, the media, the public), vertical (up and down the organization), and horizontal (with peers)."

"That sounds important, but if that's it you can still let the plan go without it in my estimation."

"That's not it!" David's pitch elevating. "There's more, lots more, to it. Communication methods that you present in your communication plan may be any combination of the following: formal (issuing reports, memos, and briefings), informal (using e-mails, ad-hoc discussions), official (using newsletters, annual reports), or unofficial (for example, off-the-record communications). You may also choose to state whether the communications will be written, oral, verbal, or nonverbal, which includes voice inflections and body language. The communication management plan documents the types of information needs the stakeholders have, when the information should be distributed, and how the information will be delivered. For example, project status, project scope statement, scope statement updates, project baseline information, risks, action items, performance measures, and deliverable acceptance."

"Calm down, man. Don't burst a gasket. Haven't you already determined the stakeholder's information needs earlier in the planning process so that, as the project team develops project-planning documents, it is clear who should receive copies of them and how they should be delivered?"

"I have that information." David's look and tone soften. "I'm not worried about that part of it. I just needed the boss not to scrap the communication plan completely. Now that he has given his blessing to proceed I know that the type of information that is presented in the communication management plan will often include a list of things. Take a look at this list." After rummaging around in his desk for a moment he whips out a list of things that a communication management plan should have, waving it in front of his colleague's face. The list reads as follows:

- stakeholder communication requirements
- information to be communicated, including language, format, content, and level of detail
- reason for the distribution of that information
- time frame and frequency for the distribution of required information
- person responsible for communicating the information
- person responsible for authorizing release of confidential information
- persons or groups who will receive the information
- methods or technologies used to convey the information, such as memos, e-mail, or press releases
- resources allocated for communication activities, including time and budget
- escalating process, identifying time frames, and the management chain for escalation of issues that cannot be resolved at a lower staff level
- method for updating and refining the communication management plan as the project progresses and develops

- glossary of common terms
- flowcharts of the information flow in the project
- communication constraints, usually derived from specific legislation or regulation, technology, and organizational policies
- guidelines and templates for project status meetings, project team meetings, e-meetings, and e-mail
- information about using a project website and project management software if they are used in the project

"You're charged up. Clearly too much energy drink at the fun run. I'd channel that energy into writing the communication plan if I were you. You're looking at another all-nighter."

"Don't be a smart aleck. I'm worried."

"I know you are. I'll cover for you here. Go home now and do what you have to do."

David leaves.

JJ Enterprises—Communication Plan

Project Name:	JJ Enterprises Records Management	
Prepared by:	Project Manager	
Date:	June 20XX	

1. Project Purpose
To develop and implement a robust system inclusive of a set of documented rules based on conventional standards of records management. This improved system is intended to replace the records management system presently in place within JJ Enterprises fifteen locations.

2. Overarching Program Objectives
The revamped records management system at JJ Enterprises is intended to • create a records classification system where individual records are arranged according to the record activity (use) or the importance of particular records or both;

	• develop a system that facilitates the proper creation, utilization, retention, transfer, and disposal of records; and • provide adoption procedures for records storage and retrieval based on prescribed rules and procedures.
3.	**Communication Approach and Principles**
	Communication will be • straightforward and honest in keeping with JJ Enterprises values and standards for two-way communication; • consistent to all stakeholder groups and/or audiences; • written in a conversational tone; • concise, direct, and produced in a manner that is easily understood to be mindful of the time constraints of the audience; and • timely and cost effective to reflect user preference.
4.	**Communication Objectives**
	• Ensure that everyone understands and knows the respective process steps and measurement components associated with the revamped records management system. • Promote and explain the benefits of the revamped records management system at JJ Enterprises. • Clarify the roles of the respective stakeholders. • Gain support and cooperation for the initiative, informing stakeholders how and where they fit into the process. • Promote two-way discussion and face-to-face communication as a means of increasing acceptance and sustaining change.
5.	**Target Audience For Communication Messages**
	• Jason and Jamina McKenzie • records management staff • general staff at JJ Enterprises
6.	**Key Messages**
	• Filing and retrieval of records as it relates to records classification and the records cycle is done with ease. • The design of the records classification system will focus on the record activity or use and the importance of records. • The records storage and retrieval system at JJ Enterprises will be revamped. • A robust records management system inclusive of a set of documented rules based on conventional standards for records management will be developed and implemented.
7.	**Change Implications**
	This initiative represents change for JJ Enterprises and the staff given that it represents something new. Outlined below is the nature of the change in terms of the following.

How the new method(s) differ from what employees are used to doing
- The idea of storing and retrieving records is not new to JJ Enterprises. The only thing that may be new here is the improved method that is more structured and organized.

How behaviors and practices have to change
- Formal records management conventions must be integrated into daily work.
- Records management staff must apply the formal records-management convention for ease in storage and retrieval of records.
- The automated system must be used without exception.
- Employees must adhere to deadlines that relate to completion of inputting data and retrieving information.
- Workers must use suspension open-shelf files for computer printouts.
- Staff must use classifying records according to their activity or use and importance.
- Employees must implement the new practices, which relate to creating, using, retaining, transferring, and disposing of records.
- Staff must commit to using the new records management system according to the rules for full benefit.
- Individuals must be open to enhanced work with teams.
- Team-building activities may be required to build cohesion.

Expectations that will have to change
- Initial time dedicated to completing work tasks may increase initially as the staff member becomes acquainted the new system.
- Approach to completing assignments and preparing records will require greater structure.
- Individualistic approach to work needs to be combined with teamwork. The program promotes the full engagement of all stakeholders.

How stakeholders can participate in and even shape the change through communication
- Identify clear milestones to check that all work that relates to the implementation and management of the records management system is completed on schedule.
- Ensure that all stakeholders are fully engaged by communicating the benefits and solicit feedback.
- Create focus groups to surface concerns and build enthusiasm.
- Continue to look for and embrace opportunities to sell project in fun settings and contexts.
- Be proactive in gaining commitments for resources when they are needed.
- Provide as much training on the new processes as practical, as early as possible.

- Train anyone who needs to install, use, or support any aspect of the records management system.
- Encourage respective persons to read the weekly status reports to communicate progress against assigned work plan activities.
- Schedule status meetings to keep people informed of project status.
- Organize team-building activities for cohesion.
- Ensure that all policies, practices, and processes are current and documented so that everyone is aware of the requirements as they relate to the revamped records management system.
- Communicate precisely how the new processes differ from the old ones.
- Communicate potential changes as far in advance as possible.
- Use the communication plan to keep all stakeholders engaged and informed.
- Be open to input from all stakeholders and allow them to feel that they have impact.
- Keep the sponsors engaged and ready to intervene when necessary and appropriate.
- Use consensus-building techniques when possible.

8. Challenges and Opportunities

The following may help or hinder the plans regarding communications:
- Competing demands may make it challenging to manage the schedule.
- Competing demands may make it easy for the stakeholder and team to drift apart and lose focus.
- Key resources may not be available to complete required project work.
- Expectations may not be reasonable for what can be accomplished within time and budget.
- Stakeholders may not readily give of their time to provide the information and support that revamped records management system requires.
- Stakeholders may undermine and work against the project.
- Approvals and sign-off on project documents may be cumbersome and lengthy.
- All stakeholders may not readily embrace and welcome the new initiative and will not sign off on or approve the key documents that must be approved for the project to progress.
- The timing for the program may be bad as it may be competing with other initiatives that are being rolled out in JJ Enterprises.
- Staff may not have sufficient time to complete their daily work as well as the requirements of the records management system during the migration phase.

Audience	Message	Channel	Responsible	Delivery Date
Jason and Jamina McKenzie	• introduction letter advising of course requirement • initial meeting to discuss and secure buy-in • meetings to discuss needs analysis and sign-off • meetings to discuss design document and sign-off • meetings to review developed content and sign-off • meetings to discuss analyzing the recommended system, assessing the recommended system for capacity and expansion, and supporting the recommended filing arrangement • weekly status reports • roll-out details	• letter • face-to-face meetings • e-mails • conference calls	Project manager	As required
Staff at JJ Enterprises	• introduction letter advising of initiative to revamp records management system • initial meeting to discuss program and secure buy-in • project sponsor update	• letter • face-to-face meetings • e-mails	Jason and Jamina McKenzie and the project manager	
Programmer	• request for proposal based on the design document and the project statement of work • meeting with prospective vendors at a bidder's conference	• letter • face-to-face meetings • e-mails	Procurement department Jason and Jamina McKenzie	As required

Audience	Message	Channel	Responsible	Delivery Date
	• references from qualified vendor • review of bids from eligible vendors for hardware, platform, data conversion, custom modules, and training • awarding of contract • initial meeting to discuss system and secure buy-in • meetings to discuss system development and sign-off • status reports update • implementation details • train-the-trainer sessions		Programmer Project manager	
Records management department team	• introduction letter advising of initiative • initial meeting to discuss revamped records management system and secure buy-in • building expectations • implementation details • weekly status report • meetings regarding change requests • results of change-control requests • weekly team meeting • conference calls with stakeholders • management updates	• letter • e-mails • face-to-face meetings • tele-conference calls • posters/ flyers/ notices	Jason and Jamina McKenzie Project manager	As required

9. Project Communication Plan Signatures			
I have reviewed the information contained in the project communication plan and agree.			
Name	Role	Signature	Date

Assess the Risk

Flipping the pages of the latest edition of a popular project management magazine, David happens on an article on risks that piques his interest. The article is presented as follows: risks, as they say, are ever-present in our lives, and a project is no exception.

"What is a risk?" you may ask. A risk is an uncertain event or condition that, if it occurs, has an effect on at least one project objective. Objectives may include scope, schedule, cost, and quality. A risk event may have one or more causes, and if it occurs, it may have one or more impacts. A cause may be a requirement, an assumption, a constraint, or a condition that creates the possibility of a positive or negative outcome.

Risk causes may include, for example, the requirement of an environmental permit to perform work or having limited personnel assigned to design the project. You should apply the principles of project risk management to all projects and must include these principles in project plans and operational documents. Risk management addresses uncertainty in project estimates and assumptions. The more you know about risks and their impacts beforehand, the better equipped you are to handle a risk when it occurs.

Not all risks are bad. They may present future opportunities as well as future threats to the project. Known risks are the ones that you identified and analyzed, making it possible to respond promptly to those risks. Unknown risks, on the other hand, cannot be managed proactively, which suggests that you and your project team should create a contingency plan. When a risk event occurs, it ceases to become uncertain.

When you conduct your risk management planning, you are really defining how you will conduct activities to manage risk in your project. Your risk management plan ensures that the appropriate amount of resources and the appropriate time are dedicated to risk management. Planning is important to provide sufficient resources and time for risk management activities. You also need to establish an agreed-upon basis for evaluating risks. Your risk management planning process should begin as soon as your project is conceived and should be completed early during project planning.

As previously mentioned, you should be conscious of risks from the point of project conception. You should always be mindful of risks as you gather information to prepare project documents, some of which you may be familiar with. For example, let's take a look at the project scope statement, which provides a clear sense of the range of possibilities associated with the project and its deliverables. Your project scope statement establishes the framework for how significant your risk management effort may ultimately become.

Your project cost documents, which define budgets, contingencies, and management reserves, also include risk-related information that you should be mindful of. Your project schedule should include contingencies that should be reported and assessed, as should your communication plan. Your communication plan should always be clear about who will be available to share information on various risks and responses at different times and locations.

Your plan to communicate information that relates to risks should be based on your stakeholders' risk attitudes and tolerances or the degree of risk that they are willing to accept. Risks that are threats to your project may be accepted if the risks are within tolerances and are in balance with the rewards that may be gained by taking the risks. For example, adopting a fast-track schedule is a risk taken to achieve the reward created by an earlier completion date.

A risk cannot be managed unless it is first identified. After you have created a plan for managing risk, your next step should be to identify the risks. This is an ongoing process aimed at identifying all the knowable risks to project objectives.

Your objective should be to identify risks to the maximum practicable extent. At the time when you identify the risk, you may also identify potential responses. As you record the possible responses, you should determine the instances where immediate action is appropriate.

If you have project plans, assumptions, and historical information from previous projects, you should review these documents from the total project perspective as well as from the perspective of individual deliverables and activity levels. Reviewing documents in this way should help you and your project team identify risks associated with the project objectives.

You may also brainstorm with and interview subject matter experts, team members, stakeholders, customers, and people with previous experience on similar projects or with specialized knowledge or industry expertise. During these sessions, you ask the interviewees to disclose the risks that happened on similar projects and predict what may happen on your project. Sometimes it is helpful to prompt the experts to dig deeper than the risk itself and look at the causes of the risks. This helps to define the risks more clearly and also helps later when you are developing a strategy to respond to the risk.

One of your goals for identifying risks is to come away with sufficient information to build a list of the risks that you identify. The risks should be described in as much detail as is reasonable in the risk register. Your goal is not only to create a list with all of the risks that you identify; you also need to have considered the root causes of those risks. You are well advised at this point to also include a list of potential responses next to the risks that you identify in the risk register. The risk register ultimately contains the outcomes of the other risk management processes as they are conducted. This results in an increase in the level and type of information contained in the risk register over time.

The four strategies that you may use for negative risks or threats are to avoid, transfer, mitigate, or accept.

Avoid

Risk avoidance involves changing the project management plan to eliminate the threat entirely. As project manager, you may choose to also isolate the project objectives from the risk's impact or change the objective that is in jeopardy. Examples of this include extending the schedule, changing the strategy, or reducing the scope.

Transfer

Risk transfer requires shifting some or all of the negative impact of a threat, along with ownership of the resources, to a third party. Transferring the risk simply gives another party responsibility for its management; it does not eliminate the risk. Transferring liability for risk is most effective when dealing with financial risk exposure. Insurance is one form of risk transfer. Contracting is another form of risk transfer. Contracting transfers specific risks to the vendor, depending on the work required by the contract.

The vendor accepts the responsibility for the cost of failure. Other forms of transference that you may consider include warranties, guarantees, and performance bonds. Risk transference nearly always involves payment of a risk premium to the third party taking on the risk.

Mitigate

When you mitigate risk, you attempt to reduce the probability of a risk event and its impacts to an acceptable level. Seeing the risk ahead of time allows you to reduce the threat by planning ways around it or planning ways to reduce its impact if the risk does occur. Taking early action to reduce the probability or impact of a risk occurring on your project is often more effective than trying to repair the damage after the risk has occurred.

Examples of mitigating risks include performing more tests, using less-complicated processes, using prototypes, and using more reliable vendors.

Accept

The acceptance strategy is used when you are not able to eliminate all of the threats on your project. Acceptance of a risk event is a strategy that may be used for risks that pose either threats or opportunities to your project. Passive acceptance is a strategy that means that you won't make any plans to avoid or mitigate the risk. You are willing to accept the consequences should they occur. Passive acceptance requires no action at all other than to document the strategy, leaving the project team to deal with the risks as they occur.

Acceptance may also mean that the project team is unable to come up with an adequate response strategy and must accept the risk and its consequences. Active acceptance might mean developing contingency reserves to deal with the risks should they occur. The most common active-acceptance strategy is to establish a contingency reserve, including amounts of time, money, or resources to handle the risks.

The acceptance strategy indicates that the project team has decided not to change the project management plan to deal with a risk or that they are unable to identify any other suitable response strategy.

Another method for planning risk responses is to consider strategies for positive risks or opportunities. The four strategies for positive risks or opportunities are to exploit, share, enhance, and accept.

Exploit

When you exploit a risk event, you are looking for opportunities for positive impacts. This is the strategy of choice when you have identified positive risks that you want to make certain will occur on your project. This strategy seeks to eliminate the uncertainty associated with a particular upside risk by ensuring that the opportunity definitely happens. An example of directly exploiting responses is assigning an organization's most talented resources to the project to reduce the time to complete or to provide lower costs than originally planned.

Share

The share strategy is similar to the transfer strategy. Here you assign the risk to a third-party owner who is best able to bring about the opportunity the risk presents. For example, perhaps your organization does great at investing but is not so good at marketing. Forming a joint venture with a marketing firm to capitalize on a positive risk will make the most of the opportunities. Other examples are risk-sharing partnerships, teams, or special-purpose companies. Sharing a positive risk involves allocating some or all of the ownership of the opportunity to a third party for the benefit of the project.

Enhance
The enhance strategy closely watches the probability or impact of the risk event to ensure that the organization realizes the benefits. This entails watching for and emphasizing risk triggers and identifying the root causes of the risk to help enhance impacts or probability. Examples of enhancing opportunities include adding more resources to an activity to finish early.

Accept
Accepting an opportunity is being willing to take advantage if it comes along but not actively pursuing it.

A contingent response strategy is another technique that you may use when planning your risk response. Contingency planning involves planning alternatives to deal with the risks should they occur. This is different from mitigation planning in that mitigation looks to reduce the probability of the risk and its impact.

Contingency planning does not necessarily attempt to reduce the probability of the risk and its impact; contingency planning says the risk might very well occur and you'd better have plans in place to deal with it when it does. Contingency comes into play when the risk event occurs. This implies that you need a plan for your contingencies well in advance of the threat occurring.

After you identify and quantify your risks, you should develop contingency plans and keep these plans ready. Events that trigger the contingency response include missing immediate milestones or gaining a higher priority with a supplier. Contingency allowances or reserves are a common contingency response. Contingency reserves include project funds that are held in reserve to offset any unavoidable threats to project schedule, cost, or quality. They also involve reserving time and resources to account for risks.

You should consider stakeholder risk tolerances when determining the amount of contingency reserves. Fallback plans should also be developed for risks with high impact or for risks with identified strategies that might not be the most effective at dealing with risk.

Sample Risk Register

Project Title: Cadet Training   **Date Prepared:**   June 20XX

Risk ID	Risk Statement	Probability	Impact					Score	Response
			Scope	Quality	Schedule	Cost			
ID	Description of the risk event or circumstances	Likelihood of occurrence	Impact on each objective if it does occur					Probability X impact	Description of planned response strategy to the risk event.
1	Senior officers may not be receptive to the change that comes along with the recommendations.	0.5			5	5		2.5	
2	Training officers may not be willing to change old behaviors.	0.7		7	7			4.9	Be open to input from the staff on process changes for better ideas and allow them to feel they have impact. Create an aggressive communication plan to keep training officers engaged and communicate the benefits of the program.
3.	Training officers and staff may revert to old behaviors after the project has been completed and integrated into daily operations.	0.7		7	7	7		4.9	Secure employee buy-in and commitment. Ensure that they know how to use the process as well as the consequences for not using it. Closely manage behaviors through reinforcement and rewards after implementation.

Risk ID	Risk Statement	Probability	Impact				Score	Response
			Scope	Quality	Schedule	Cost		
ID	Description of the risk event or circumstances	Likelihood of occurrence	Impact on each objective if it does occur				Probability X impact	Description of planned response strategy to the risk event.
4.	Some training officers and staff may feel threatened by the change	0.7		7	7	7	4.9	Ask for stakeholder participation in planning and requirements gathering. Reassure that the change is for the better and secure buy- in.
5.	The training officers and staff may not be monitored after the project transitions into operations and as such they may not adhere to the new training procedures.	0.8		8	8	8	6.4	Appoint a champion with responsibilities for reinforcing the program postimplementation as well as to ensure proper application of the maintenance plan. Ensure that the champion has the full support of senior officers. Include a system for rewarding and recognition.
6.	Learning curve with training officers and staff may result in lower initial productivity.	0.8		8			6.4	Provide as much training on the new processes as early as possible.

Risk ID	Risk Statement	Probability	Impact					Score	Response
			Scope	Quality	Schedule	Cost			
ID	Description of the risk event or circumstances	Likelihood of occurrence	Impact on each objective if it does occur					Probability X impact	Description of planned response strategy to the risk event.
7.	Some stakeholders may undermine or work against the project.	0.8		8	8	8		6.4	Ask for stakeholder participation in planning and requirements gathering.
8.	The budget in terms of man hours may not be realistic.	0.7	7	7	7	7		4.9	Recalculate the project cost estimates.
9.	Substantial change in processes may result in destructive behavior.	0.5			5	5		2.5	
10.	Uncertainty may cause decisions to be delayed.	0.7		7	7	7		4.9	Be open to stakeholder input on process changes for better ideas and allow them to feel they have impact. Create an aggressive communication plan to keep stakeholders engaged and informed.
11.	It may be difficult to reach consensus.	0.8		8	8	8		6.4	Include representatives from special-interest groups when collecting requirements, performing quality assurance, and testing.

Definition of Risk-Rating/Scoring Technique

The project will rate each identified risk (e.g., Impact Score = High, Medium, Low) based on the likelihood that the risk event will occur and the effect on the project's objectives if the risk event occurs. This will be a subjective evaluation based on the experience of those assigned to the project's risk management team.

Default Rating/Scoring System

Impact Score can be rated as 1, 3, 5, 7, or 9 (1=Very Low, 9=Very High). Probability may be rated as 0.1, 0.3, 0.5, 0.7, or 0.9 (0.1=Very Low, 0.9=Very High).

Risk Thresholds

The project team will establish risk responses for risk events that have been determined to have a rating of High. Risk priority is determined by calculating a risk score (Impact x Probability) and then comparing that risk score to priority thresholds. Based on the scoring system, the lowest possible risk score is 1 x 0.1 = .01, and the highest possible risk score is 9 x 0.9 = 8.1.

The following priority thresholds will be used to establish risk priority:
Green (Low Risk) < 2.5
Yellow (Medium Risk) between 2.5 and 6.5
Red (High Risk) > 6.5

- The project team develops a full response plan for each item rated as **High** risk. These risks are watched closely.
- The project team should create a response plan for any **Medium** risk item where they deem it necessary; however, in general no response plan is required for Medium risk items. Medium risks are monitored on a regular basis.
- No action is required for **Low** risk items except to keep a watch on them as the project progresses.

All risks with a response plan are to be entered into the risk-register document.

Make or Buy

It's late in the evening, and David is on his way home from another long day at work, drained and hungry. He has decisions to make: does he stop at the grocery store, buy some raw ingredients, go home, slave over the stove, and wait at least another hour before he eats, or does he stop off and get some food on the go?

Oddly enough, the make-or-buy decision on the subject of his dinner is like the make-or-buy decisions made on a project as it relates to purchasing or acquiring products and services. Project-procurement management includes the processes necessary to purchase or acquire products, services, or results needed from outside the project team. The organization may be either the buyer or the seller of the products, services, or results of the project.

Managing contracts and purchase orders is included as a part of David's procurement management responsibilities. Contracts are legal documents between the buyer and the seller. Procurement contracts are legally binding and may include terms and conditions as well as other items that the buyer specifies to establish what the seller is to perform or provide. As project manager, it's David's responsibility to ensure that all procurements meet the specific needs of the project while adhering to the organization's procurement policies.

In planning project-procurement activities, David decides to use the procurement management plan as a template for new projects similar to the one that he is currently managing. He is planning to prepopulate the fields with the company's processes. Users can then fill in the information specific to their projects in the future.

A preamble on the template may prove helpful for newcomers to the field of project management. The preamble begins by explaining that planning project-procurement activities includes identifying potential sellers and documenting the approach and the purchase decisions as they relate to the project. When conducting procurement planning, identify those project needs that must be fulfilled for which it is necessary to acquire products, services, or results outside the organization.

When thinking about whether or not to acquire outside support, consider what needs to be acquired, how it will be acquired, how much of it needs to be acquired, and when it should be acquired. Consider who is responsible for obtaining or holding any relevant permits and professional licenses that may be required by legislation, regulation, or organizational policy in executing the project. The project schedule requirements may significantly influence your strategy for planning procurements. The scope statement describes the need for the project and lists the deliverables and acceptance criteria for the product or service of the project. Consider assumptions that relate to the reliability of the vendor. Assuming that key resources will be available and that there will be adequate stakeholder involvement may impact the decisions made as they relate to planning procurements.

The product scope description included in the project scope statement may alert you to special considerations, such as the services, technical requirements, and skills needed to produce the product of the project.

The work-breakdown structure and the work-breakdown structure dictionary identify the deliverables and describe the work required for each element of the work-breakdown structure.

The risk register, which includes risk-related information such as the identified risks, risk owners, and risk responses, may serve as a guide for determining the types of services or goods needed for procurement. Consider the risks involved with each make-or-buy decision. This information may impact the type of contract that is used with respect to mitigating risks or sometimes transferring risks to a seller. Risk-related contract decisions include agreements such as insurance, bonding services, and other items as appropriate that are prepared to specify each party's responsibility for specific risks as they relate to the project's procurement activity.

Activity-resource requirements that contain information on specific needs such as people, equipment, or location as well as the project schedule may be used when planning procurements. The schedule contains information on the time lines of mandated delivery dates. This information is important to have when planning procurements. Activity-cost estimates developed by procurement activity are used to evaluate how reasonable potential seller bids or proposals are. This information works in conjunction with the cost-performance baseline, which provides detail on the planned budget over time.

Consider requirements with contractual and legal implications, which may include health, safety, security, performance, environmental, insurance, intellectual property rights, equal employment opportunity, licenses, and permits. All of these elements should be considered when planning procurements.

Sometimes two or more vendors may form a legal contractual agreement to work together in partnership or as a joint venture on a particular project. If teaming agreements are used on a project, typically the scope of work requirements for competition, buyer and seller roles, and other important concerns should be predefined. Whenever the new business opportunity ends, the teaming agreement also ends.

Consider conducting a make-or-buy analysis when planning procurements. A make-or-buy analysis asks whether it is more cost effective for a particular work to be accomplished by the project team or purchased from outside sources. Sometimes capacity may exist within the organization but may be committed to working on other projects. In this case, the project may need to source effort from outside the organization to meet its scheduled commitments.

Costs should include both direct and indirect costs. The buy side of the analysis includes both the actual out-of-pocket costs to purchase the product and the indirect costs of supporting the purchasing process and purchased item. In other words, direct costs include the actual cost to purchase the product or service and indirect costs such as ongoing maintenance costs.

Costs don't necessarily mean the cost to purchase. In make-or-buy analysis, the cost of leasing items versus the cost of buying them may also be considered.

Other considerations in make-or-buy analysis include elements such as capacity issues, skills, availability, and trade secrets. Strict control may be necessary for a process that cannot be outsourced. Budget constraints may also influence make-or-buy decisions. Consider the use of expert judgment when planning project-procurement activities. Expert judgment may also be used to develop or modify the criteria that will be used to evaluate seller proposals.

Expert judgment may involve the services of legal staff to assist with unique procurement issues, terms, and conditions. Such judgment, including business and technical expertise, may be applied to both the technical details of the acquired product, services, or results and to various aspects of the procurement management processes.

David considers including a "types of contract" section in the template that he is creating. This section is intended to state that all equipment and material purchases require fixed-price contracts. When human resources are required for the project on a contract basis, a time-and-material contract should be used with the unit rates stated in the contract. He recommends that a "not to exceed" amount should also be written into the contract to avoid surprises regarding the total amount of dollars that the company will be charged for the resources. For this information to make sense to the template user, David decides to build the following explanation on contract types into the template preamble.

There are three different types of contracts included in this category:

1. Fixed price
2. Cost reimbursable
3. Time and material

Fixed Price or Lump Sum

Fixed-price contracts may be disastrous for both the buyer and the seller if the project scope is not well defined or if the scope changes dramatically. On the other hand, this type of contract may be relatively safe for both the buyer and the seller when the original scope is well defined and remains unchanged.

If you are leaning toward the use of this contract type, it is important that you have well-defined deliverables. Fixed-price contracts typically reap only small profits for the seller and force the contractor to work productively and efficiently. This type of contract also minimizes cost and quality uncertainty.

Cost-Reimbursable Contracts

Cost-reimbursable contracts are as the name implies. The allowable costs defined in the contracts that are associated with producing the goods or services are charged to the buyer.

All the costs the seller takes on during the project are charged back to the buyer, and thus the seller is reimbursed. Cost-reimbursable contracts carry the highest risk to the buyer, because the total costs are uncertain. As problems arise, the buyer has to shell out even more money to correct the problems.

The advantage to the buyer with this type of contract is that scope changes are easy to make and can be made as often as you want—but it will cost you. This category of contract involves payments (i.e., cost reimbursements) to the seller for *all* legitimate actual costs incurred for completed work *plus* a fee representing the seller's profit. Cost-reimbursable contracts may also include financial-incentive clauses whenever the seller exceeds or falls below defined objectives, such as costs, schedule, or technical-performance targets.

Cost-reimbursable contracts have lots of uncertainty associated with them. The contractor has little incentive to work efficiently or become productive. This type of contract protects the contractor's profit, because increasing costs are passed to the buyer rather than taken out of profits, as would be the case with a fixed-price contract. Cost-reimbursable contracts are used most often when the project scope contains a lot of uncertainty, such as for cutting-edge projects and research and development. They are also used for projects with large investments early in the project life.

Time-and-Material Contracts

Time and material contracts are a cross between fixed-price and cost-reimbursable contracts. The full amount of the material costs is not known at the time when the contract is awarded.

This aspect resembles a cost-reimbursable contract, because the costs will continue to grow during the contract's life and are reimbursable to the contractor. The buyer bears the biggest risk in this type of contract. The full value of the agreement and the exact quantity of the items to be delivered may not be defined by the buyer at the time of the contract award.

Time-and-material contracts may also increase in contract value as if they were cost-reimbursable contracts. Many organizations require that not-to-exceed values and time limits be placed in all time-and-material contracts to prevent unlimited cost growth. Time-and-material contracts may resemble fixed-price contracts when certain parameters are specified in the contract, such as unit rates for material or labor. These rates are often preset and agreed upon by the buyer and the seller ahead of time. These rates may also include the seller's profits when both parties agree on the values for specific resource categories, such as a senior engineer at specified hourly rates or categories of materials at specified rates per unit. Time-and-material contracts are most often used when human resources with specific skills are needed and when you can quickly and precisely define the scope of work for the project.

David includes contract type calculations in the template preamble for the convenience of new users.

Fixed-Price Incentive-Fee Contracts

1. **If the ceiling price is $120,000, target cost is $100,000, target profit is $10,000, target price is $110,000, and share ratio is 70/30, how much should the seller receive if the actual costs are $80,000?**
    Ceiling Price = $120,000
    Target Cost = $100,000
    Target Profit = $10,000
    Target Price = $110,000
    Share Ratio 70/30

    Formula
    Actual Costs + Target Profit + Share of Savings

    Scenario
    *   If actual costs exceed ceiling price, seller receives no extra profit and buyer pays ceiling price only.

• If actual costs ($80,000) are less than target costs ($100,000) seller receives 30 percent of the $20,000 savings plus other fees.

Applying the Formula
Actual Costs + Target Profit + Share of Savings
$80,000 + $10,000 + $6,000 = $96,000.

2. **The ceiling price is $300,000, target cost is $200,000, target profit is $50,000, target price is $250,000, and share ratio is 40/60. If actual costs are $200,000, what do you pay the seller?**
Ceiling Price = $300,000
Target Cost = $200,000
Target Profit = $50,000
Target Price = $250,000
Share Ratio 40/60

Formula
Actual Costs + Target Profit + Share of Savings

Scenario
• If actual costs are $200,000, what do you pay the seller?

Applying the Formula
Actual Costs + Target Profit + Share of Savings
$200,000 + $50,000 = $250,000.

3. **If the ceiling price is $300,000, target cost is $200,000, target profit is $50,000, target price is $250,000, and share ratio is 40/60, what will you pay the seller if the actual costs are $280,000?**
Ceiling Price = $300,000
Target Cost = $200,000
Target Profit = $50,000
Target Price = $250,000
Share Ratio 40/60

Formula
Actual Costs + Target Profit + Share of Savings

Scenario
• If actual costs are $280,000, what do you pay the seller?

Applying the Formula
Actual Costs + Target Profit + Share of Savings
$280,000 + $50,000 =$300,000

Cost-Plus-Fixed-Fee Contracts

4. **If the cost ceiling is $90,000, the fixed fee is $9,000, and the value of the total contract is $99,000, how much will you be reimbursed by if you spend $120,000?**

Cost Ceiling = $90,000
Fixed Fee = $9,000
Total Contract Value = $99,000

Formula
Cost Ceiling + Fixed Fee

Scenario
• How much will you be reimbursed by if you spend $120,000?

Applying the Formula
Cost Ceiling + Fixed Fee
$90,000 + $9,000 = $99,000

5. **If the cost ceiling is $90,000, the fixed fee is $9,000, and the value of the total contract is $99,000, how much will you be reimbursed by if you spend $80,000?**

Cost Ceiling = $90,000
Fixed Fee = $9,000

Total Contract Value = $99,000

Formula
Cost Ceiling + Fixed Fee

Scenario
• How much will you be reimbursed by if you spend $80,000?

Applying the Formula
Cost Ceiling + Fixed Fee
$80,000 + $9,000 = $89,000

Cost-Plus-Incentive-Fee Contracts

6. **If the expected cost is $100,000, the initial fee to the seller is $10,000, the final cost is $80,000, and the share ratio is 85/15, what amount will the seller receive? What amount will the buyer receive?**

   Expected Cost = $100,000
   Initial Fee to Seller = $10,000
   Final Cost = $80,000
   Share Ratio 85/15

   Applying the Formula—Determining What the Seller Receives
   Final Costs + Initial Fee + Share Ratio * Savings
   $80,000 + $10,000 + .15 * $20,000 = $93,000

   Applying the Formula—Determining What the Buyer Receives
   Share Ratio * Savings
   .85 * $20,000 = $17,000

7. **If the expected cost is $200,000, the initial fee to the seller is $40,000, the final cost is $180,000, and the share ratio is 60/40, what will the seller receive?**

Expected Cost = $200,000
Initial Fee to Seller = $40,000
Final Cost = $180,000
Share Ratio 60/40

Applying the Formula—Determining What the Seller Receives
Final Cost + Initial Fee + Share Ratio * Savings
$180,000 + $40,000 + .40 *20,000 = $228,000

8. **If the expected cost is $200,000, the initial fee to the seller is $40,000, the final cost is $210,000, and the share ratio is 60/40, what will the seller receive?**

Expected Cost = $200,000
Initial Fee to Seller = $40,000
Final Cost = $210,000
Share Ratio 60/40

Applying the Formula—Determining What the Seller Receives
Final Cost + Initial Fee + Share Ratio * Savings
$210,000 + $40,000 = $250,000

Manage Your Stakeholders

Inevitably your project plan will impact your stakeholders positively and sometimes negatively. As a project manager, David finds that he must continuously create effective ways of keeping stakeholders engaged in the project, managing the expectation he has for them and their expectations for him. The project's ultimate goal is to achieve the project's objectives, and given that the project is undertaken to meet a need, demand, or concern that was unearthed by stakeholders, it stands to reason that stakeholders are front of mind.

Stakeholder management is really about relationship building as a means of satisfying stakeholders' needs and concerns in the context of the project.

With the project management plan and subsidiary plans complete and e-mailed to the boss for vetting, David feels that he has accomplished a great deal. Two milestone documents complete—what an achievement! But there's still much work to be done, and with the deadline fast approaching, David moves to project executing, monitoring, and controlling.

Key Points to Remember

The Project Manager

- Success or failure on a project all comes down to leadership.
- The project manager may play the role of a guide, an influencer, a consensus builder, an observer, a peacemaker, a taskmaster, an empathetic listener, an encourager, and a documenter. A project manager should understand people, communicate effectively, influence what others think, and facilitate healthy conflict resolution.
- Knowledge of existing organizational structure, personnel policies, and technical, interpersonal, and political factors must be considered when planning and managing a project.
- Skills like networking, relationship building, influencing, and team leadership are critical when identifying and documenting project roles.
- A project manager should demonstrate important skills like active listening and effective questioning and probing ideas and situations.

Plan Your Project

- A project management plan is the document that governs the way the project will be managed.
- The project management plan may be inclusive of several subsidiary plans that provide greater detail around how certain processes should be performed.
- The project management plan must always be current and reflect the most recent updates.

- Information from the project charter is used when creating a project management plan. Therefore, it is very important to write a project charter when initiating a project.

Scope out Your Project

- Write down all requirements in sufficient detail that you or anyone else can measure these requirements once the project work begins.
- Interviews, questionnaires, and survey information from customers may be used to obtain requirements information.
- Grouping requirements into categories helps for better organization.
- Linking stakeholders to specific requirements helps to ensure that requirements that are important to specific stakeholders are met.
- Product scope refers to the features and characteristics that describe the product, service, or result of the project.
- Project scope describes the project management work, and the scope statement documents the project's objectives, tangible outcomes, and the work required to produce these tangible outcomes.
- Exclusions are anything that is not included as a deliverable or work of the project.
- Constraints are anything that either restricts the actions of the project team or dictates the actions of the project team.
- The WBS defines and organizes the project work and includes 100 percent of the work defined by the project scope.
- Support each element of the project scope by an activity or activities that will result in the completion of the work.

Scheduling

- Defining activities document the specific activities needed to fulfill the requirements detailed in the project scope.

- The description of each activity should begin with a verb, and a single person should be responsible for performing the activity.
- Once the activities are defined and listed, they should be sequenced.
- Initial activity sequencing should not include resource availability.
- The four types of logical relationships are finish-to-start, finish-to-finish, start-to-start, and start-to-finish.
- Resources are typically the largest expense on a project and do not include only people but may also include equipment and supplies.
- Activity-duration estimates are quantifiable estimates expressed as the number of work periods needed to complete a scheduled activity.
- Work periods may be expressed in hours, days, or even months.

Let's Talk Money

- You are required to develop cost estimates for all resources required for each scheduled activity.
- Some alternatives that you may consider include make versus buy, buy versus lease, and sharing resources across projects or departments.
- Information from the scope statement, the work-breakdown structure (WBS), the work-breakdown structure dictionary, and the project schedule may be used when estimating costs.
- Market conditions and regional or global supply-and-demand conditions may also influence costs.
- Information that relates to labor rates, material costs, inflation, and risk factors is valuable data when estimating costs.
- Reviewing records from previous projects that are similar in scope, cost, budget, and duration to the one that you are presently working on is a good way of obtaining valuable data used to estimate costs.

- Reserve analysis is a technique that may be used to account for cost uncertainty.
- Add up all the cost estimates of the activities to determine the total budget.
- The cost-performance baseline is a measurement tool for your project.

Don't Forget Quality

- Quality typically defines whether stakeholder expectations were met.
- Identify quality requirements or standards for the project and product when planning quality.
- Quality planning should take place in conjunction with other planning processes.
- Information on quality may be obtained from the scope statement, the stakeholder register, and the risk register.
- Government agency regulations, rules, standards, and guidelines specific to the application area and working or operating conditions of your project or product may also provide insight on quality requirements.
- Cost-benefit analysis is an approach that can be used to obtain the information that you need to plan quality.
- Consider the trade-off of the cost of quality. It is cheaper and more efficient to prevent defects in the first place than to spend time and money fixing them later.
- The cost of quality is the total cost to produce the product or service of the project according to the quality standards.
- Three costs associated with the cost of quality are prevention costs, appraisal costs, and failure costs.
- Appraisal costs are the costs that you incur to examine the product or process.
- Failure costs are what it costs when things do not go according to plan.
- Internal failure costs result when customer requirements are not satisfied while the product is still in your control.

- External failure costs occur when the product has reached the customer and the customer determines that the requirements are not met.

Getting Good People

- The activity-resource requirements can be used to determine the human resources needs.
- Consider the availability of resources, skill levels, and training needs in order to develop the human resources plan.
- The staffing management plan, which is produced as a part of developing the human resources plan, describes how and when human resources requirements will be met.
- The staffing management plan must be continually updated.
- The staffing management plan provides information on staff acquisition, release, and rewards and recognition.

Effective Communication is Key

- The communication plan should document the approach that you will take to ensure efficient and effective communication with your stakeholders.
- Effective communication means that information is provided in the right format at the right time and with the right impact.
- Efficient communication means that you provide only the information that is necessary.
- The communication plan may represent communication over several dimensions and may use any combination of communication methods.
- Listening, questioning, and negotiating are communication skills that may be used on all projects.
- You should determine the communication needs of the stakeholders early in the planning process so that, as the project team develops project-planning documents, it is clear who should receive copies of them and how they should be delivered.

Assess the Risk

- A risk is an uncertain event or condition that, if it occurs, has an effect on at least one project objective.
- Project objectives may include scope, schedule, cost, and quality.
- A risk event may have one or more causes, and if it occurs, it may have one or more impacts.
- Not all risks are bad; risks may present future opportunities as well as future threats to the project.
- When a risk event occurs, it ceases to become uncertain.
- When you consider your risk management planning, you are really defining how you will conduct activities to manage risk on your project.
- Your risk management plan assures that the appropriate amount of resources and the appropriate time are dedicated to risk management.
- Your risk management planning process should begin as soon as your project is conceived.
- Risk-related information may be obtained from the project scope statement, project cost documents, project schedule, and your communication plan.
- A risk cannot be managed unless it is first identified.
- Identifying risks is an ongoing process.
- Brainstorming and interviewing subject matter experts, team members, stakeholders, customers, and people with previous experience on similar projects are great ways to collect high-quality information about risks.
- One of your goals for identifying risks is to come away with sufficient information to build a list of the risks that you identified, where the risks are described in as much detail as is reasonable.
- Four strategies that you may use for negative risks or threats are to avoid, transfer, mitigate, or accept.
- Four strategies that you may use for positive risks or opportunities are to exploit, share, enhance, and accept.

Make or Buy

- Project-procurement management includes the processes necessary to purchase or acquire products, services, or results needed from outside the project team.
- The organization may either be the buyer or seller of the products, services, or result of the project.
- Contracts are legal documents between the buyer and the seller.
- Planning your procurement activity includes identifying potential sellers and documenting the approach and the purchase decisions as they relate to the project.
- When determining whether to acquire outside support or not, consider what needs to be acquired, how it will be acquired, how much of it needs to be acquired, and when it should be acquired.
- It is important to consider who is responsible for obtaining or holding the relevant permits and professional licenses that may be required by legislation, regulation, or organizational policy in executing your project.
- The scope statement, the WBS, the WBS dictionary, the risk register, risk-related contract decisions, activity-resource requirements, activity-cost estimates, the cost-performance baseline, requirements documentation, teaming agreements, and the project schedule are all documents that you should consult when planning your project-procurement needs.
- Conducting a make-or-buy analysis when planning procurement should be considered.
- The use of expert judgment when planning your project-procurement activities should be considered.
- Expert judgment may involve the services of legal staff to assist with unique procurement issues, terms, and conditions.
- Fixed price or lump sum, cost reimbursable, and time and material are all examples of contract types.

Manage Your Stakeholders

- It is important to develop strategies to effectively engage and manage stakeholders throughout the life of the project based on their needs, interest, and potential impact on project success.

Applying to the Next Project

Discussion Questions

1. What is a project manager? Why is a project manager important?
2. What knowledge and skills does a project manager need to have?
3. What behavior does a project manager need to demonstrate?
4. How does a project manager apply knowledge and skill in and out of project settings?
5. Why do you need steps to follow when planning a project? What are those steps?
6. What is meant by the baseline?
7. What is meant by collecting requirements? And why is this important on a project?
8. What are some ways that you can go about collecting requirements?
9. How do you categorize and prioritize requirements?
10. Why is it important to understand what is included in or excluded from a project?
11. What are the steps in creating a WBS?
12. What would be the benefit of breaking down all of the project work into work packages?
13. What is meant by activities?
14. Why is completing all activities related to each work package on a project important?
15. What does the process of sequencing activities entail?

16. How do you determine what resources you may need to complete each activity?
17. How do you determine how long it will take to complete each activity?
18. What documents are produced as a result of scheduling?
19. What is meant by project costs?
20. Why is completing all activities related to each work package on a project important to determine project costs?
21. What are some ways that you may go about costing activities?
22. How do you determine what budget you may need to complete each activity?
23. What options may be available if you run out of money on a project?
24. What documents are produced as a result of project costing?
25. What is meant by quality? Why is it important to complete all project activities in a way that promotes quality?
26. What does the process of ensuring quality entail?
27. How can you follow the steps for ensuring quality?
28. How do you determine what quality requirements are necessary to complete each activity?
29. Who are the persons responsible for ensuring quality, and what may their respective roles in the project be?
30. Why is it important to plan for human resources?
31. What does the process of assigning people to project activities entail?
32. Who is responsible for ensuring that human resources are assigned to respective project activities?
33. What may happen if there is no plan to bring people on and take them off of a project?
34. What may happen to your project if the human resources are not assigned to the appropriate activity?
35. What is meant by a project communication plan? Why is completing a project communication plan important?
36. What does the process of completing the project communication plan entail?
37. What may happen in the absence of effective communication?

38. What document is produced as a result of communication planning?
39. What type of information is included in the communication plan?
40. What is meant by project risk?
41. What impact may risk have on a project? Why is it important to properly identify risks on a project?
42. What may potentially happen if you fail to properly identify risks on a project?
43. What are some ways that you may go about identifying risks on a project?
44. What are some strategies for addressing negative risks or threats? Positive risks and opportunities?
45. What is the document that is produced as a result of identifying risks in a project?
46. What is meant by procurement?
47. Why are contracts and purchase orders necessary when planning the procurement requirements for the project?
48. What is included as a part of planning procurement activities?
49. What should be some consideration when determining whether or not to acquire products, services, or results from outside of the organization to meet the project requirements?
50. What are some documents that may be used to provide insight on the project-procurement requirements?
51. Why should you consider conducting a make-or-buy analysis?
52. Why should you include experts when making decisions that relate to your project-procurement plans?
53. Who are some of the experts that you may use when making decisions that relate to your project-procurement plans?
54. What are the three contract types?
55. Which contract type may potentially reap the greatest rewards for the seller?
56. Which contract type requires a well-defined scope and deliverables?
57. What are the characteristics of a time-and-material contract?

Debrief Questions

1. What are the key learning points?
2. What information was new to you?
3. What concepts will you apply in the future? When?
4. What challenges do you anticipate may limit your ability to apply the concepts?
5. What needs to be in place to overcome these challenges?
6. Who would you recommend these concepts to and why?

Activity

The following activity may be completed individually or in a small group to assess your comprehension.

1. Answer the discussion questions.
2. Answer the debrief questions.
3. Use the completed templates presented in the chapter to create project-planning documents for a project of your own.
3. Review previous projects where project-planning documents were inaccurate or not comprehensive. Discuss the outcome in those instances.

Chapter 3

Work Hard and Follow Up

After studying this chapter, you should be able to accomplish the following:

- explain what is meant by acquiring the team
- describe the kind of information that you may obtain from the human resources plan that may assist you in acquiring the project team
- list and describe those events that might occur in the external environment that may impact your ability to acquire the project team
- state the kind of information that may be obtained from within the organization that may assist with acquiring the project team
- list and describe four methods that may be used when acquiring the project team
- describe the importance of rewarding and recognizing the project team
- cite the ways that information may be presented to stakeholders on a project
- discuss some documents that may be used to assist with understanding the way information should be distributed on a project
- list and describe some communication methods that support the process of distributing information on a project
- explain the connection between group size and conflict-resolution techniques
- describe the variety of ways that project information may be distributed
- examine the six elements for inclusion in stakeholder notification

- describe what is meant by the term "managing stakeholder expectations"
- examine the purpose of the issues log and the change log
- explain the importance of monitoring and controlling the project
- list and describe some activities that may be included as a part of monitoring and controlling the project
- list and describe some results of monitoring and controlling the project
- explain what is meant by verifying the scope
- discuss the importance of scope verification
- state what is meant by controlling scope
- explain the importance of controlling scope
- explain what is meant by controlling the schedule
- describe what is included as a part of cost control
- examine the purpose of earned-value management
- summarize what is included as a part of earned-value management
- discuss the documents that may be used to obtain information for reporting project performance
- explain the importance of performance reports
- state the importance of monitoring and controlling risks
- explain how risks are monitored and controlled in a project

---

David prepares to chair the stakeholder meeting. Waiting for the meeting to begin, he mentally conducts a high-level review of the agenda, thinking about what he intends to discuss with the group. He intends to accomplish the following:

- welcome the group to the meeting
- inform the group that the project is in executing
- outline the following tasks that must be completed as a part of project execution:

    o   acquiring the project team
    o   developing the project team (ongoing process)
    o   distributing information
    o   requesting seller responses
    o   selecting sellers
    o   performing quality assurance (ongoing process)

- inform the group of the tasks included as a part of project execution, which are completed to-date:
  - requested seller responses
  - selected sellers
- inform the team that the purpose of the meeting is to distribute and discuss the information that relates to the project

David's name is announced, and it's his turn to speak. He thanks the team for attending the meeting and communicates the message above, which he spent the last five minutes formulating in his head. After expressing excitement that the project is in execution, he proceeds to review the following items:

- project milestones included in the project scope document
- project schedule, highlighting dates of critical importance
- the communication schedule included in the project communication plan

Given that the launch date is fast approaching, David spends considerable time discussing the communication schedule outlined in the project communication plan with particular emphasis on the following items:

- purpose for the communication events
- audience
- channel
- responsibility for communicating the message
- delivery date

David gains consensus and stakeholder buy-in for the roles that they will play in ensuring a successful project launch. He concludes by updating the team on the following:

- the vendor's progress with developing and testing
- the vendor's progress with developing step-by-step instructions for use of system functionality
- his own progress

The meeting ends, and David and the team return to work.

Acquire Your Team

David slumps over his desk, forehead cupped in his hands, reflecting on the current state of his project and thinking about how he will get the right people on his project team. He is tired of being turned down for the high-quality staff and being forced to accept what he deems "the misfits." He imagines the star performers calling him and begging him to accept them as a part of the project team. How can he make this dream a reality? A familiar voice interrupts his thoughts in the midst of conjuring a response.

"David, do you have a minute? Something's on my mind,"

"How can I help you, Debbie?"

"I just heard through the grapevine that Yvette's assigned to work on the project team. I'm just letting you know, David, that if this is true, I'm off the team. I can't work with Yvette. She's loud, obnoxious, mouthy, and full of attitude."

David thinks for a moment and then responds, "Debbie, I want you to work on this project; it's a great opportunity. Yvette is a solid performer and an ace instructional designer. Without Yvette's talent we'd blow the budget and time estimates established for this project."

"David, I'm telling you: if I have to work with Yvette I'll be crushed, and I'll snivel and cry day after day on this project. I'm not at my best when I am disappointed."

"Debbie, I need both you and Yvette. It's important to get the right people assigned to the project team. We can't afford to hire from outside for this project. I've been told no contract help. Here's what I propose: I'll clearly outline roles and responsibilities for all team members in the kick-off meeting. At that time I'll also clearly state that negative team interactions will not be allowed."

"So what if I have a problem with Yvette that I can't resolve on my own? I need you to get involved and take care of it, David."

"I'll take care of it, Debbie. I promise. I'll take care of it."

"Thanks. I know you will."

As project manager, it's David's job to ensure that resources are available and skilled in the project activities to which they are assigned.

Here's where the human resources plan comes in as a primary-source document. The human resources plan provides information that may be used as a guide for how the project's human resources may be identified, staffed, managed, controlled, and eventually released from the project. The human resources plan that David created for the project includes information like the following:

- roles and responsibilities, defining the positions, skills, and competencies that the project demands
- project organization charts indicating the number of people needed for the project
- staffing management plan outlining the time period each project team member will be needed as well as other information important to acquiring the project team

Events happening in the external environment that may influence acquiring the project team include and are not limited to

- existing information for human resources, including who is available, their competency levels, their prior experience, their interest in working on the project, and their cost rate;
- human resources policies, such as those that affect outsourcing;
- organizational structure; and
- location or multiple locations.

Organizational standard policies, processes, and procedures may also influence acquiring the project team.

Several methods may be used for acquiring the project team, including preassignment, negotiation, acquisition, and virtual teams.

Preassignment may happen when the project is put out for bid and specific team members are promised as part of the proposal. Preassignment may also happen when internal project team members are promised and assigned as a condition of the project. When staff members are promised as part of the project proposal—particularly on internal projects—they should be identified in the project charter.

Negotiation is a common technique used to ensure that the project receives appropriately competent staff in the required time frame and that the project team members will be able, willing, and authorized to work on the project until their responsibilities are completed. Negotiation may also be used to support and encourage team members to remain on the team, as was the case with David and Debbie.

The project management team may need to negotiate with other project management teams within the performing organization to appropriately assign scarce or specialized human resources. The project management team may also need to negotiate with other project management teams within the external organization, vendors and suppliers, contractors, and so on for appropriate, scarce, specialized, qualified, certified, or other human resources. Special consideration should be given to external negotiating policies, practices, processes, guidelines, legal, and other such criteria. The project management team's ability to influence others plays an important role in negotiating staff assignments, as does the politics of the organization involved.

Acquisition is another method that may be used to secure project team members. When the performing organization lacks the in-house staff needed to complete a project, the requested services may be acquired from outside sources. This may involve individual consultants or subcontracting work to another organization. The availability of electronic communications such as e-mail, audio conferencing, web-based meetings, and videoconferencing has made virtual teams feasible. A virtual team does not necessarily work in the same location. They have little or no time spent face-to-face, but their members all share the goals of the project and have roles to fulfill. Virtual teams allow for the inclusion of persons from different geographic locations, those who work different hours or shifts than the other team members, those with mobility limitations, and so on.

Communication planning is increasingly important in a virtual team environment. Additional time may be needed to set clear expectations, facilitate communications, develop protocols for resolving conflict, include people in decision making, and share credit in successes.

Project team members need the right environment, where they can feel a sense of pride in doing the work that they enjoy. The ground rules that David committed to Debbie in order to support a harmonious relationship between her and Yvette helps to create the right working environment. A strong alignment between the basic components of the job and the employee's talents and strengths also helps to create the right work environment for project team members to find internal rewards from the work itself.

Project team member recognition and rewards do not necessarily have to be costly. At the same time, the types of recognition and rewards that team members receive should be things that they believe justify the time, effort, and mental and emotional sacrifice that they put into their work.

It is a known fact that people are different. As such, a reward or recognition that may be effective to one team member may not necessarily be effective for another. To be effective, rewards and recognition should be aligned with the project team member's values.

Rewards and recognition should not only be aligned with project team members' values but should also align to the organization's values. Sometimes organizations capture their values in the form of mission statements, vision statements, core values, and the like. Then the organization circulates these written values among employees, customers, and the external community.

David involves the project team members as much as possible in designing and developing the rewards-and-recognition program that is associated with the project. He finds out from the project team members what they value and, as much as possible, aligns rewards and recognition to these values.

"Recently the team's been working lots of overtime and some weekends to meet their deliverables, and they have been successful. I dedicate this time slot on this stakeholder meeting agenda to bring my team to the forefront and praise them for their cooperation and efforts in meeting their deliverables. As I call each team member's name, come forward and I will present you with three days paid time off and a gift certificate for two at the all-inclusive day spa." The room erupts in applause.

David rewards and recognizes project team members in ways that mean something to them. The reward criteria was clearly stated and known to all team members. Every team member who met the required criteria was rewarded and recognized.

Distribute Information

"I need help," Yvette says to David, hearing the desperation in her own voice.

David looks at her. He appears dog tired, his eyes bloodshot with dark circles. He looks like she feels, and that's not good.

"Hi, Yvette, I'm glad you stopped by," he says, motioning toward his coffee cup. "I was going to give you a call first thing in the morning, because I've been trying to reach you for days. I really need a briefing on the stakeholder's reaction to the information that you distributed last week." David rubs his hands wearily over his eyes.

"Actually, I'm ashamed to admit it, but I forgot to distribute the project information to the stakeholders last week. I know that I should have told you sooner, but I just could not build up the courage to bring it to your attention." David's ruddy complexion blushes shades of burgundy. His heart sinks.

"Surely you can relate to the feeling of being the last one told about an important event or situation that directly affects you. This is not a good feeling, especially if it is a situation where we may have prevented an outcome or reduced the consequences of some actions had I known about this important information in advance. You do realize that failing to ensure that the right information is distributed to the people on the project can bring the project to a screeching halt, leaving us all standing alone in the dirt.

"What do I need to know?" He begins writing on a blank page in his day-planner notebook.

Yvette weighs the pros and cons of truth and lying and decides to give David the benefit of the truth. David smiles; it's not a pretty expression … more ominous than joyful.

"We're in big trouble." David's voice is monotone as he considers the situation. He knows that distributing project information is the process of making relevant information available to project stakeholders as planned. This may come about in several ways, such as the following:

- status reports
- project meetings
- review meetings

Performing the process of distributing project information should occur throughout the entire project life cycle and in all management processes. The focus here is mainly in the execution process, which includes implementing the communication management plan as well as responding to unexpected requests for information.

"What held you back from distributing the information, Yvette?" David asks without even a trace of enthusiasm in his voice.

"I am not educated about the process," she confesses warily.

"If you're wondering how to go about distributing project information, here are some helpful hints. The communication plan tells you how the project-related information is to be distributed and the specific timing around that process. There are also performance reports. Performance reports used to distribute project performance and status information should be made available prior to the project meetings and should be as precise and current as possible. Forecasts are updated and reissued based on work-performance measurements provided as the project is executed. Information about the project's past performance may impact the project in the future.

"Have you accessed the templates from the shared drive?"

"The what?"

"You don't know about the templates? The organization's policies, procedures, and guidelines regarding information distribution may also influence the way project information is distributed. Always use templates, historical information, and lessons learned. They are available to you on the shared drive."

"Oh, yeah. That thing. I didn't know what it was called, but yeah, I've seen it."

"Yeah," he says, adding a tremendous amount of sugar to his coffee. "I'll go on to explain a bit about communication methods and skills to help educate you on the process of distributing project information." David covers his mouth with his hands and coughs. Once his hacking fit is under control, he begins his explanation.

"Communication methods include all means feasible to communicate project information to the proper recipients, such as meetings, e-mail, videoconferences, conference calls, and so on. Communication skills are arguably one of the most important skills you can have, even more important than technical skills. Good communication skills foster an open, trusting environment a best asset.

"Information exchange involves a sender, a message, and a receiver.

Sender

"The sender is the person responsible for putting the information together in a clear and concise manner. The information should be complete and presented in a way that the receiver will be able to correctly understand. The message should be relevant to the receiver.

Message

"The message is the information being sent or received. It may be written, verbal, nonverbal, formal, informal, internal, external, horizontal, or vertical. Horizontal communications are messages sent to and received from peers. Vertical communications are messages sent to and received down to subordinates and up to executive management.

Receiver

"The receiver is the person for whom the message is intended. The receiver is responsible for understanding the information correctly and making sure that he or she receives all the information. Receivers filter the information that they receive through their knowledge of the subject, culture, influences, language, emotions, attitudes, and geographic locations. The sender should take these filters into consideration when sending messages so that the receiver will clearly understand the message that was sent. Senders, receivers, and messages are the elements of communication.

"Shall I continue, or am I going over information that for you is redundant?"

"This is all new for me."

"Didn't Debbie tell you all of this in the briefing?"

Yvette's mouth pops open. "What briefing? I never had any briefing with Debbie."

David, too tired to respond, raises his chin a couple of notches and continues with a controlled tone.

"The way the sender packages or encodes the information and transmits it and the way the receiver unpacks or decodes the message are the methods of communication exchange. Senders encode messages. Encoding is a method of putting the information into a format the receiver will understand. Language, pictures, and symbols are used to encode messages. Encoding formats the message for transmitting. Transmitting is the way the information gets from the sender to the receiver. Spoken words, written documentation, memos, e-mail, and voice mail are all transmitting methods.

"Decoding is what the receiver does with the information when he gets it. He converts it into an understandable format. Usually this means that he reads the memo, listens to the speaker, reads the book, and so on. Communication occurs primarily in written or verbal form. Verbal communication is easier and less complicated than written communication and is usually a faster method of communication. Written communication, on the other hand, is an excellent way to get across complex, detailed messages.

"Detailed instructions are better provided in written form because it gives the reader the ability to go back over information that they are not sure about. Both verbal and written communication might take a formal or an informal approach.

"Group size makes a difference when trying to resolve a conflict or make a decision. The larger the group, the more lines of communication and the more difficult it will be to reach a decision. Groups of five to ten people have a manageable number of participants and have been shown to make the most accurate decisions. If your team and your stakeholders trust that you can communicate the vision and the project goals and report on the project status accurately and honestly, you will most likely be successful.

"An information-distribution tool is the final tool and technique required for distributing information. Project information may be distributed using a variety of tools, including

- hard-copy document distribution, manual filing systems, press releases, and shared-access electronic databases;
- electronic communication and conferencing tools, such as e-mail, fax, voice mail, telephone, video and web conferencing, websites, and web publishing; and
- electronic tools for project management, such as web interfaces to scheduling and project management software, meeting and virtual office support software, portals, and collaborative-work-management tools.

"This feels a bit like a monologue. Am I boring you?"

"Quite the contrary," Yvette says. "I'm taking it all in. Although I'm not asking any questions, I'm absorbing it all. I never knew anything about distributing project information. I appreciate you taking the time to explain all of this to me. Continue."

He looks doubtful but nods anyway. "Okay, I'll spare no detail. I don't what to take any unnecessary chances." He glances at his watch inconspicuously. "There are six elements that should be included as a part of distributing information to keep stakeholders informed of project activity: stakeholder notification, project reports, project presentations, project records, feedback from stakeholders, and lessons-learned documentation.

"Stakeholder notifications involve notifying the stakeholders when you have implemented solutions and approved changes, updated project status, resolved issues, and so on. Project reports include project status reports and minutes from project meetings, lessons learned, closure reports, and other documents from all the process outputs throughout the project. If you are keeping an issue log, the issues would be included with the project reports as well.

"Project presentations involve presenting project information to the stakeholders and other appropriate parties when necessary. The presentations might be formal or informal and depend on the audience and the information being communicated. Project records include memos, correspondence, and other documents concerning the project. The best place to keep information like this is in a project notebook or in a set of project notebooks depending on the size of the project. The project notebooks are ordinary three-ring binders where project information gets filed. They are managed by the project manager or project office and contain all information regarding the project. This information may also be backed up in the company intranet, on a project website, or on CDs.

"Individual team members might keep their own project records as well, in notebooks or electronically. These records serve as historical information once the project is closed.

"Feedback received from the stakeholders that may improve future performance on projects may be captured and documented. If the information has an impact on the current project, distribute it to the appropriate team members so that future project performance may be modified to improve results.

"Lessons learned are information that you gather and document throughout the course of the project and that may be used to benefit the current project, future projects, or other projects currently being performed by the organization. Lessons learned may include positive as well as negative lessons.

"During the process of distributing information, you will begin conducting lessons-learned meetings focusing on many different areas depending on the nature of the project. These areas might include project management processes, product development, technical processes, project team performance, stakeholder involvement, and so on.

"Lessons-learned meetings should always be conducted at the end of project phases and at the end of the project at a minimum. Team members, stakeholders, vendors, and others involved on the project should participate in these meetings. It is important to understand and to make team members aware that lessons-learned meetings are not intended to be finger-pointing experiences. The purpose of the lessons-learned meetings is to understand what went well and why, so it may be repeated for future projects, and what did not go well and why, so that it may be performed differently on future projects.

"The meetings can create team-building sessions because an atmosphere of trust and sharing may be created while building on each other's strengths to improve performance. The reasons or causes for the issues or the corrective action taken should be documented as well as any other information that future projects may benefit from."

"So where does that leave us?" Yvette says, inching toward the exit.

"It leaves us," David says, "at the point of scheduling a meeting at 8:00 a.m. tomorrow to craft an action plan and agree to next steps."

She sighs. "I was thinking we could talk more tonight."

"Oh, well, I didn't have anything else to do tonight … like sleep, or anything boring like that. Tomorrow morning, 8:00 a.m. We'll address it then."

Manage Expectations

"We can squeeze a seat for you over here in the holding room. You know it's standing room only, but we are trying to accommodate everyone," the hostess whispers hurriedly.

The no-frills cubicle-sized enclosure referred to as the "holding room" was designed to give invited guests that claustrophobic feeling. And it was most effective. With nothing to look at but the beige paint on the walls, nothing to sit on but the white aluminum folding chairs, and the temperature raised to at least thirty degrees above normal room temperature, occupants had that snug cozy feeling usually associated with being in a crowded elevator.

"Raise your spirits, buddy," David hears an unfamiliar voice call out. "Just concentrate on the keynote speaker and you'll soon get outta here."

He turns toward the voice, one eyebrow raised. "Thanks. Knew there was some reason why I opted to be here." Instantly he turns serious, taking in the information on managing stakeholder expectations.

Managing stakeholder expectations is the process of communicating and working with stakeholders to meet their needs and address issues as they occur. Managing stakeholder expectations involves communication activities directed toward project stakeholders to influence their expectations, address concerns, and resolve issues. This may include

- actively managing stakeholders' expectations to increase the likelihood of project acceptance;
- addressing concerns that have not become issues yet, usually related to the anticipation of future problems;
- uncovering and discussing concerns and assessing risks; and
- clarifying and resolving issues that have been identified.

The resolution may result in a change request or may be addressed outside of the project, for example, postponed for another project or phase or deferred to another organizational entity. Managing expectations helps to increase the probability of project success by ensuring that the stakeholders understand the project benefits and risks.

This enables stakeholders to be active supporters of the project and to help with risk assessment of project choices. By anticipating people's reactions to the project, preventive actions may be taken to win their support or minimize potential negative impacts. The project manager is responsible for managing stakeholder expectations. Actively managing stakeholder expectations decreases the risk that the project will fail to meet its goals and objectives due to unresolved stakeholder issues. It also limits disruptions during the project.

An issue log or action-item log may be used to document and monitor the resolution of issues. It may be used to facilitate communication and ensure a common understanding of issues.

Issues do not usually rise to the importance of becoming a project or activity but are usually addressed in order to maintain good, constructive working relationships among various stakeholders, including team members. The issues are clearly stated and categorized based on urgency and potential impact. An owner is assigned an action item for resolution, and a target date is usually established for closure. Unresolved issues may be a major source of conflict and project delays.

A change log is used to document changes that occur during a project. These changes and their impact to the project in terms of time, cost, and risk must be communicated to the appropriate stakeholders.

PROJECT ISSUE—Details							
Project Name:							
Project Manager:							
Instructions: • *Log in each issue request as it is received.*							
Request No.	Link to Project Issue Document	Issue Description and Impact to Project	Priority (H,M,L)	Reported By	Status	Date Resolved	Resolution / Comments

Project Issue Document

Use this document to report significant issues in your project:

- Record details about the issue in section 1.
- Document the result of analysis in section 2; e.g., will resolution have impact on project cost or schedule?
- Record recommendations in section 3 and final management decision in section 4.

Project Name:	
Prepared By:	
Date:	
1. Issue Background	
Fill in with appropriate information or place an "X" next to those that apply.	
Issue Type:	
Request for Information ( ) Procedural Problem ( ) System Problem ( ) Other ( )	
Issue Description:	
Potential Impact (if not resolved):	
Attachments (if any) No ( ) Yes ( )	
Date Resolution Needed:	
2. Analysis	
Reviewer Name:	
Review Completion:	
Reviewer Comments:	

Initial Recommendation:

Cost/Schedule Impact Analysis Required? Yes ( ) No ( )

Proposed Assignee:

Estimate of Additional Effort

Resources Required	Work Days/Costs

3. Recommendation

Final Recommendation and Comments

Name	Title	Signature	Date

4. Management Action

Recommendation Status: Fill in with appropriate information or place an "X" next to those that apply.

Accept ( ) Defer ( ) Reject ( ) Need Additional Information ( )

Assigned to:

Planned Completion Date:

Name	Title	Date	Comment

5. Project Issue Document Signatures			
Project Manager:			
Name	**Title**	**Signature**	**Date**

Sample Status Report

Project Title:	JJ Enterprises Records Management	**Date Prepared:**	June 20XX

Team Member:	John Doe	**Role:**	Project Manager

Activities Planned for This Reporting Period June 14–June 17, 20XX:

1. Conduct needs analysis.
2. Review the records practices currently in use in JJ Enterprises.
3. Review the need for more human resources in the area of records management and make appropriate recommendation if necessary based on the proposed records management and filing arrangement.
4. Complete project-initiating documents, including project charter, stakeholder register, and stakeholder management strategy.

Activities Accomplished This Reporting Period:

1. Conduct needs analysis (completed).
2. Review records practices currently in use at JJ Enterprises (completed).
3. Review the need for more human resources in the area of records management and make appropriate recommendation if necessary based on the proposed records management and filing arrangement (submitted proposal to Jason and Jamina McKenzie on June 14, 20XX and expect to receive feedback on June 17, 20XX).

Activities Planned but Not Accomplished This Reporting Period:

1. Complete project-initiating documents, including the project charter, and stakeholder register. (The project charter is complete, and the stakeholder register will be completed by June 16, 20XX; sign-off on all of these documents will not be completed until June 18, 20XX.)

Root Cause of Variances:

The cause of the variance for any work that was not accomplished:
- Stakeholders were not available to provide relevant information.
- Records management staff were not available to provide source data.
- Time allocated was insufficient to complete the required amount of work as the project documents took longer to complete than was originally anticipated.

Funds Spent This Reporting Period:

US$10,000 was spent during this reporting period.

Funds Planned to Be Spent This Reporting Period:

US$5,000 was planned to be spent during this reporting period.

Root Cause of Variances:

The root cause of the cost variance was limited to labor and not material. This variance was as a result of not having access to the relevant source data and extra time spent preparing project documents. Errors had to be corrected, and this took extra time and money.

Quality Variances Identified This Period:

There are no quality variances identified during this period.

Planned Corrective or Preventive Action:

Actions needed to recover cost and schedule variances or prevent future variances include ensuring that the resources are available in advance and that the necessary research is conducted in advance of when it is necessary to be included in the project documents.

Activities Planned for Next Reporting Period June 17–June 20, 20XX

1. Complete stakeholder register document.
2. Sign off on project-initiating documents.
3. Sign off on project plan inclusive of subsidiary plans.
4. Create design documents of the records management system that is recommended to address the deficiencies in the present system.
5. Sign off on design document of records management system.
6. Begin to produce project executing and monitoring and controlling documents.

Costs Planned for Next Reporting Period:

$US15,000.

New Risks Identified:

- Time allocated for respective activities may be insufficient if access to resources and source documents is unavailable.
- Some incomplete items from the previous period are now carrying over into current period. This will require more time and possibly resources to complete.
- These risks are recorded in the risk register.

Issues:

- Issues that have arisen this period include insufficient access to resources and source documents.
- There was inappropriate time allocation.
- These issues will be recorded in the issue log.

Comments:

Ensure that any change requests that may be required to address project variances are processed through the proper channels and corresponding project documents are updated accordingly.

Change Log

Project Title: Records Management System   **Date Prepared:** June 20XX

Change ID	Category	Description of Change	Submitted by	Submission Date	Status	Disposition
01	Cost Variance	Additional US$3,000 for completion of project-initiation documents WBS 1.1.2.1	John Doe	June 16, 20XX	Closed	Approved

Project Lessons-Learned Checklist

Project Name:	
Prepared By:	
Date	

Use this lessons-learned checklist as an aid to understanding those factors that either helped or hindered the project. It is best used in a group discussion among those who have a stake in the project but may be used at any time as a discussion tool or during the project close as a part of the lessons-learned exercise.

1.	**Project Lessons-Learned Checklist**								
Instructions: **Yes** = The project team agrees with the statement. **No** = The project team does not agree with the statement. **N/A** = This statement does not apply to the project. **Impact** = The extent to which this factor had an impact on your project.									
No.		**Yes**	**No**	**N/A**	**Impact**				
					Low			**High**	
					1	2	3	4	5
1.	Business objectives were specific, measurable, and attainable; results focused; and time limited.								
2.	Product concept was appropriate to business objectives.								
3.	Project plan and schedule were well documented with appropriate structure and detail.								
4.	Project schedule encompassed all aspects of the project.								
5.	Tasks were adequately defined.								
6.	Stakeholders (e.g., sponsor, customer) had appropriate input into the project-planning process.								

7.	Requirements were gathered in sufficient detail.										
8.	Requirements were documented clearly.										
9.	Specifications were clear and well documented.										
10.	Design documents were adequate, understandable, and well documented.										
11.	External dependencies were identified and agreements signed.										
12.	Project budget was well defined.										
13.	End-of-phase criteria were clear for all project phases.										
14.	Project plan had buy-in from all stakeholders.										
15.	Stakeholders had easy access to project plan and schedule.										
	Project Execution and Delivery										
16.	Project stuck to its original goals.										
17.	Changes in direction that did occur were of manageable frequency and magnitude.										
18.	Project baselines (scope, time, cost, and quality) were well managed (e.g., changed through a formal change-control process).										
19.	Design changes were well controlled.										
20.	Basic project management processes (e.g., risk management, issue management) were adequate.										
21.	Risks were managed.										
	Human Factors										
27.	Project manager was effective.										
28.	Project team was properly organized and staffed.										
29.	Project team's talent and experience were adequate.										

30.	Project team worked effectively on project goals.									
31.	Project team worked effectively with outside entities.									

1.	**Project Lessons Learned Checklist Cont.**

Instructions:
Yes = The project team agrees with the statement.
No = The project team does not agree with the statement.
N/A = This statement does not apply to the project.
Impact = The extent to which this factor had an impact on your project.

No.		Yes	No	N/A	Impact				
					Low			High	
					1	2	3	4	5
32.	There was good communication within the project team.								
33.	Management gave this project adequate attention and time.								
34.	Resources were not overcommitted.								
35.	Resources were consistently committed to project teams.								
36.	Functional areas cooperated well.								
37.	Conflicting department goals did not cause problems.								
38.	Authority and accountability were well defined and public.								
	Overall								
39.	Initial cost and schedule estimates were accurate.								
40.	Product was delivered within amended schedule.								
41.	Product was delivered within amended budget.								
42.	Overall change control was effective.								

43.	External dependencies were understood and well managed.									
44.	Technology chosen was appropriate.									
45.	Customer's needs/requirements were met.									
46.	Customer was satisfied with the product.									
47.	Product objectives were met.									
48.	Business objectives were met.									

2. Project Lessons-Learned Checklist—Agreement Form/Signatures			
Project Name:			
Project Manager:			
I have reviewed the information contained in this Project Lessons-Learned Checklist and agree:			
Name	Title	Signature	Date

Monitor and Control Your Project

David doesn't see anyone at first. He just sees the number of e-mails in his inbox and the number of voice messages on his phone. The sight makes his knees grow weak. How do you like the "welcome back from vacation" wagon?

You may be familiar with the saying that when the cat's away, the entire operation goes awry. Well, that's a modified version of the saying, but I'm sure you get the point. The moral is, if you leave something, or someone for that matter, too long unattended, things tend to become unwieldy.

Monitoring and controlling the project work is the process of tracking, reviewing, and regulating the progress to meet the performance objectives defined in the project management plan. This includes measuring project performance to identify variances from the project plan and get the project back on track should things get out of hand.

Monitoring includes collecting, measuring, and distributing project information and assessing measurements and trends to effect project improvement. Continuous monitoring gives the project team insight into the health of the project and identifies any areas that may require special attention.

Control includes determining corrective or preventive actions or re-planning and following up on action plans to determine if the actions taken resolved the performance issue. The monitoring and controlling project work is concerned with the following:

- comparing actual project performance against the project management plan
- assessing performance to determine whether any corrective or preventive actions are indicated and then recommending those actions as necessary
- identifying new risks and analyzing, tracking, and monitoring existing project risks to make sure the risks are identified, their status is reported, and appropriate risk-response plans are being executed
- maintaining an accurate, timely information base concerning the project's product(s) and their associated documentation through project completion
- providing information to support status reporting, progress measurement, and forecasting
- providing forecasts to update current cost and current schedule information
- monitoring implementation of approved changes as they occur

Change requests may need to be issued as a result of comparing planned results to actual results and may expand, adjust, or reduce project or product scope. Changes may impact the project management plan, project documents, or product deliverables. Changes may include but are not limited to corrective action, preventive action, and defect repair.

Corrective action is a documented direction for executing the project work to bring expected future performance of the project work in line with the project management plan.

Preventive action is a documented direction to perform an activity that may reduce the probability of negative consequences associated with project risks.

Defect repair is the formally documented identification of a defect in a project component, with a recommendation to either repair the defect or completely replace the component.

Your project management plan may more than likely need updating as a result of monitoring and controlling the project work. The areas of your project management plan that you may update include but are not limited to the following:

- schedule management plan
- cost management plan
- quality management plan
- scope baseline
- schedule baseline
- cost-performance baseline

You will also need to update some project documents as a result of your monitoring and controlling activities. The project documents that may be updated include but are not limited to the following:

- forecasts
- performance reports
- the issue log

The integrated change-control process serves as an overseer, so to speak, of the monitoring and controlling processes. This is where you establish the project's change-control process. Change requests may come about during project execution. These change requests may include the need for corrective actions, preventive actions, and defect repair.

Changes may be requested by any stakeholder involved with the project. Although changes may be initiated verbally, you should insist that they are always recorded in written form and entered into the change-management or configuration-management system. Change requests are subject to the process specified in the change-control and configuration-control systems.

Those change-request processes may require information on estimated time impacts and estimated cost impacts. Every documented change request must be either approved or rejected by some authority within the project management team or an external organization.

On many projects, as is the case with David's project, the project manager is given authority to approve certain types of change requests as defined in the project's roles-and-responsibilities documentation. Sometimes, a change-control board may be required to approve or reject change requests. The roles and responsibilities for these boards are clearly defined within the configuration- control and change-control procedures and are agreed upon by appropriate stakeholders.

Many large organizations provide for a multitiered board structure, separating responsibilities among the boards. If the project is being provided under a contract, then some proposed changes may need to be approved by the customer, as per the contract.

Changes come about on projects for many reasons. As project manager, it is David's responsibility to manage these changes and see to it that organizational policies regarding changes are implemented. Changes do not necessarily mean negative consequences. Changes may produce positive results as well.

It is important that this process is managed carefully, because too many changes—or even a single significant change—will impact cost, schedule, scope, or quality.

Once a change request is submitted, you have some decisions to make: Should the change be implemented? If so, what is the cost to the project in terms of project constraints (cost, time, scope, and quality)? Will the benefits gained by making the change increase or decrease the chances of project completion?

Just because a change is requested this doesn't mean that it has to be implemented. Always discover the reasons for the change to determine whether it is justifiable, and be sure to identify the cost of the change. Remember that cost can take the form of increased time.

When performing integrated change control, review all change requests, approving changes and managing changes to the deliverables. Consider the organizational policies and procedures, project documents, and project management plan during this process.

In this instance, David must ensure that the project management plan, the project scope statement, and other deliverables are maintained by carefully and continuously managing changes. This is done by either rejecting changes or by approving changes, thereby assuring that only approved changes are incorporated into a revised baseline.

Approved change requests may require new or revised cost estimates, activity sequences, schedule dates, resource requirements, and analysis of risk-response alternatives. These changes may require adjustments to the project management plan or other project management documents.

The extent to which the level of change control is applied depends on the application area, the complexity of the specific project, contract requirements, and the context and environment in which the project is performed. These include the following:

- influencing the factors that circumvent integrated change control so that only approved changes are implemented
- reviewing, analyzing, and approving change requests promptly, which is essential, as a slow decision may negatively affect time, cost, or the feasibility of a change
- maintaining the integrity of baselines by releasing only approved changes for incorporation into the project management plan and project documents
- reviewing, approving, or denying all recommended corrective and preventive actions
- coordinating changes across the entire project (e.g., a proposed schedule change will often affect cost, risk, quality, and staffing)
- documenting the complete impact of change requests

A configuration-management system with integrated change control provides a standardized, effective, and efficient way to centrally manage approved changes and baselines within the project. Configuration control is focused on the specification of both the deliverables and the processes, while change control is focused on identifying, documenting, and controlling changes to the project and the product baselines.

Project-wide application of the configuration-management system, including change-control processes, accomplishes three main objectives:

1. It establishes an evolutionary method to consistently identify and request changes to established baselines and to assess the value and effectiveness of those changes.
2. It provides opportunities to continuously validate and improve the project by considering the impact of each change.
3. It provides the mechanism for the project management team to consistently communicate all approved and rejected changes to the stakeholders.

The primary purpose of verifying the scope is to formally accept completed deliverables and obtain sign-off that the deliverables are satisfactory and meet stakeholder expectations. Verifying scope includes reviewing deliverables with the customer or sponsor to ensure that they are completed satisfactorily and obtaining formal acceptance of deliverables by the customer or sponsor.

Scope verification differs from quality control and is primarily concerned with acceptance of the deliverables. Quality control is primarily concerned with correctness of the deliverables and meeting the quality requirements specified for the deliverables. It is generally performed before the scope is verified.

Control Scope

The vacation that David returned from that left his legs wobbly at the sight of his accumulated workload was at an all-inclusive resort. Have you ever had the opportunity to go to an all-inclusive resort for a holiday?

I'm told that when you pay for your package, it includes room, meals, drinks, amenities, and lots of fun.

Well, project scope mirrors the all-inclusive, but without the resort component. Project scope describes the work that is required to produce the product, service, or result of the project. I am not sure if it happens in all projects, but sometimes I am told that having fun is also a requirement that should be included in the scope.

The broad product scope statement usually includes the product description, which describes the characteristics, features, and functionality of the product, service, or result. The process of controlling scope involves the following:

- monitoring the status of both the project and the product scope
- monitoring changes to the project and product scope
- monitoring work results to ensure that they match the expected outcomes

Can you recall when Greg was explaining to David about the 100 percent rule?

Greg said, "Collectively, all levels of the WBS roll up to the top so that all project work is captured and no additional work is added."

David asked, "So what happens if someone asks you to complete an activity that is not included as a part of the WBS?"

Well, in addition to Greg's answer, which was "That's an issue," what we are addressing here also answers David's question.

Any modification to the agreed-upon work-breakdown structure is considered a scope change. This means that adding or deleting activities or any modifications to the existing activities on the work-breakdown structure constitute a project scope change. Changes in product scope require changes to the project scope as well.

Let's say that one of David's project deliverables is to design a piece of specialized equipment that is integrated into the final product. Because of engineering setbacks and some miscalculations, the specialized equipment requires design modifications. The redesign of this equipment impacts the end product, or product scope. Since changes to the product scope impact the project requirements, which are detailed in the project scope document, changes to the project scope document are also required. These changes, along with the recommended corrective actions, should be processed through the integrated change-control process.

Unapproved or undocumented changes that sometimes make their way into the project are referred to as *scope creep*. Scope creep can kill an otherwise viable project. Little changes add up and eventually impact budget, schedule, and quality. Scope control is the process of monitoring the status of the project and product and managing changes to the scope baseline. Controlling the project scope ensures that all requested changes and recommended corrective or preventive actions are processed through the integrated change-control process.

Project scope control is also used to manage the actual changes when they occur and is integrated with the other control processes. Uncontrolled changes are also referred to as scope creep. Change is inevitable, thereby mandating some type of change-control process. When scope changes are requested, you should investigate all areas of the project to determine what the changes will impact. Your project team should perform estimates of the impact and of the amount of time needed to make the changes.

Sometimes, the change request is so extensive that even the time to perform an estimate should be evaluated before proceeding. In other words, if the project team is busy working on estimates, they are not working on the project. Extensive change requests could impact the existing schedule because of the time and effort needed just to evaluate the change.

Cases like these require that a determination is made to ask the change- control board to decide whether the change is important enough to allow the project team to work on the estimates. Always remember to update the stakeholders regarding the changes that are being implemented and their impacts. They will want to know how the changes impact the performance baselines, including the project costs, project schedule, project scope, and quality.

Control Schedule

Controlling the schedule is the process of monitoring the status of the project to update the project's progress and manage changes to the schedule baseline. This includes the following:

- determining the current status of the project schedule
- influencing the factors that create schedule changes
- determining that the project schedule has changed
- managing the actual changes as they occur

Performance reviews measure, compare, and analyze schedule performance, such as actual start and finish dates, percent complete, and remaining duration for work in progress. If earned-value management is utilized (see more information below on this tool), the schedule variance and schedule performance index are used to assess the magnitude of schedule variances.

An important part of schedule control is to decide if the schedule variation requires corrective action. For example, a major delay on any activity not on the critical path may have little effect on the overall project schedule, while a much shorter delay on a critical or near-critical activity may require immediate action.

Performance reviews examine elements such as start and end dates for schedule activities and the time remaining to finish incomplete activities.

Variance analysis is another technique used for controlling the schedule. Schedule-performance measurements (schedule variance and schedule performance index) are used to assess the magnitude of variation from the original schedule baseline.

The total-float variance is also an essential planning component to evaluate project time performance. Important aspects of the project schedule include determining the cause and degree of variance relative to the schedule baseline and deciding whether corrective or preventive action is required.

Control Costs

Controlling costs is the process of monitoring the status of the project to update the project budget and manage changes to the cost baseline. Updating the budget involves recording actual costs spent to date. Any increase to the authorized budget can only be approved through the integrated change-control process.

Monitoring the expenditure of funds without regard to the value of work being accomplished for such expenditures has little value to the project, other than to allow the project team to stay within the authorized funding. Thus, much of the effort of cost control involves analyzing the relationship between the consumption of project funds and the physical work being accomplished for such expenditures.

The key to effective cost control is the management of the approved cost performance baseline and the changes to that baseline. Project costs include the following:

- influencing the factors that create change to the authorized cost baseline
- ensuring that all change requests are acted on in a timely manner
- managing the actual changes when and as they occur
- ensuring that cost expenditure does not exceed the authorized funding, by period and in total for the project
- monitoring cost performance to isolate and understand variances from the approved cost baseline
- monitoring work performance against funds expended

Earned-value management is one of the most effective performance-measurement and feedback tools in project management. Earned-value management helps to clearly show objectively where a project is and where it is going, compared to where it was supposed to be and where it was supposed to be going.

Earned-value management can play a role in answering David's questions related to management that are critical to the success of his project, such as:

- Are we delivering more or less work than planned?
- When is the project likely to be completed?
- Are we currently over or under budget?
- What is the remaining work likely to cost?
- What is the entire project likely to cost?
- How much will we be over or under the budget at the end of the project?
- What is driving the significant cost and/or schedule variances?

If, when applying earned-value management to his project, it is revealed that the project is behind schedule or over budget, as project manager David may use earned-value management methodology to help identify

- where problems are occurring;
- whether problems are critical or not; and
- what it will take to get the project back on track.

As a performance-management methodology, earned-value management adds some critical practices to the project management process. These practices occur primarily in the areas of project planning and control and are related to the goal of measuring, analyzing, forecasting, and reporting cost and schedule performance data for evaluation and action by workers, managers, and other key stakeholders.

Report Performance

Imagine Yvette's emotions as she approaches David to discuss her performance at 8:00 a.m. after revealing her neglect in completing a critical task to her role on the project team. The reckoning day would come. David would find out what Yvette was (or was not) doing. When the day arrives, there's a whole lot of sweating bullets.

If you manage your project well, you wouldn't need to sweat bullets. At the same time, you do need to report on the project's performance.

In the workplace our performance is compared to the standard, and the same holds true for a project. Project-performance reporting is the process where the collection of baseline data occurs and is documented and reported. Performance reporting involves collecting information regarding project progress and project accomplishments and reporting it to stakeholders. This is what Yvette was asked to do. Additionally, she may also report this information to project team members, the management team, and other interested parties. Her failure to report to David tipped him off that the task remained pending.

Reporting may include information concerning project quality, costs, scope, schedule, procurement, and risk. It may be presented in the form of status reports, progress measurements, or forecasts. The performance-reporting process involves the periodic collection and analysis of baseline versus actual data to understand and communicate the project progress and performance as well as to forecast the project results.

Performance reports need to provide information at an appropriate level for each audience. The format may range from a simple status report to more elaborate reports. A simple status report might show performance information such as percent complete or status dashboards for each area (i.e., scope, schedule, cost, and quality). A complete report should also include forecasted project completion (including time and cost). More elaborate reports may include

- analysis of past performance;
- current status of risks and issues;
- work completed during the period;
- work to be completed next;
- summary of changes approved in the period; and
- other relevant information that must be reviewed and discussed.

These reports may be prepared regularly or on an exception basis.

As David advised Yvette, the project management plan should be reviewed in this instance. It provides information on project baselines. The performance-measurement baseline is an approved plan for the project work to which the project execution is compared, and deviations are measured for management control. The performance-measurement baseline typically integrates the scope, schedule, and cost parameters of a project but may also include technical and quality parameters.

Also use the information from project activities that is collected on performance results, such as

- deliverable status;
- schedule progress; and
- cost incurred.

Work-performance information is used to generate project-activity metrics to evaluate actual progress compared to planned progress. These metrics include and are not limited to the following:

- planned versus actual schedule performance
- planned versus actual cost performance
- planned versus actual technical performance

It is advisable to use budget-forecast information from cost control. This provides information on the additional funds required for the remaining work as well as estimates for completing total project work. Some project considerations are influenced by the internal organization in which the project operates. Some of these considerations that impact project-performance reporting activities include and are not limited to the following:

- report templates
- policies and procedures that define the measures and indicators to be used
- organizationally defined variance limits

Project-performance information should be documented and reported to the stakeholders in the form of performance reports. This requirement should be outlined in the communication management plan. Performance reports organize and summarize the information gathered and present the results of any analysis compared to the performance-measurement baseline.

Reports should provide the status and progress information at the level of detail required by various stakeholders as documented in the communication management plan. These reports may take many forms, including S-curves (cost baselines are recorded in this way), bar charts, tables, and histograms.

Control Risks

Monitoring and controlling risks involves implementing response plans, tracking and monitoring identified risks, and identifying and responding to new risks as they occur. Anticipated risks that are included in the project management plan are addressed during the life cycle of the project.

In the article that David read about risks in a popular project management journal, he learned that as project manager, he along with the members of the project team should continuously monitor the project work for new, changing, and outdated risks. The process of monitoring and controlling risks applies techniques such as variance and trend analysis, which require the use of performance information generated during project execution.

Some of the other purposes that David may have for monitoring and controlling risk are to determine if the project assumptions he made earlier in the project are still valid or if the analysis showing an assessed risk has changed or can be retired. Risk management policies and procedures must be followed. Determine whether contingency reserves of cost or schedule should be modified in alignment with the current risk assessment.

Monitoring and controlling risk may involve choosing alternative strategies, executing a contingency or fallback plan, taking corrective action, and modifying the project management plan. As project manager, David ensures that the risk-response owner reports periodically to him on the effectiveness of the plan as well as on any unanticipated effects and any correction needed to handle the risk appropriately. Monitoring and controlling risks also includes updating the organizational process assets, including project lessons-learned databases and risk management templates for the benefit of future projects.

The processes required to initiate, plan, execute, monitor, and Control the project that David is managing are complete. Now all that's left is to officially close the project.

Key Points to Remember

Acquire Your Team

- Use the human resources plan as one of your primary-source documents when acquiring the project team.
- The human resources plan should provide you with information that you may use to guide you on how your project human resources may be identified, staffed, managed, controlled, and eventually released from the project.
- Human resources policies, such as those that affect outsourcing, may influence your ability to acquire your project team.
- Four methods that you may use to acquire your project team include preassignment, negotiation, acquisition, and virtual teams.
- Preassignment may happen when your project is put out for bid and specific team members are promised as part of the proposal.
- Negotiation is a common technique that is used to ensure that the project receives appropriately competent staff in the required time frames and that the project team members will be able, willing, and authorized to work on the project until their responsibilities are completed.
- When the performing organization lacks the in-house staff needed to complete a project, the requested services may be acquired from outside sources.
- A virtual team does not necessarily work in the same location.
- Project team members need the right environment, where they can feel a sense of pride in doing the work that they enjoy.

- Project team member recognition and rewards do not necessarily have to be costly.
- To be effective, rewards and recognition should be aligned with the project team member's values.
- Rewards and recognition should also be aligned with the organization's values.

Distribute Information and Manage Expectations

- Distributing information is the process of making relevant information available to project stakeholders as planned.
- Performance reports distributing project information and status information should be made available before the project meeting and should be as precise and current as possible.
- Organizational policies, procedure, and guidelines may influence the way information is distributed.
- Communication methods include all means feasible to communicate project information to the proper recipients, including meetings, e-mails, videoconferencing, conference calls, and so on.
- It is estimated that project managers spend as much as 90 percent of their time communicating in one form or another.
- Communication skills are arguably one of the most important skills a project manager can have.
- Information exchange involves a sender, a message and a receiver.
- The sender is the person responsible for putting the information together in a clear and concise manner.
- The message is the information being sent.
- The receiver is the person for whom the message is intended.
- Senders, receivers, and messages are the elements of communication.
- Communication occurs primarily in oral or nonverbal form.
- Group size makes a difference when trying to resolve a conflict or make a decision.
- Project information may be distributed using a variety of tools.

Monitor and Control Your Project

- Stakeholders should be notified when you have implemented solutions, updated project status, resolved issues, and so forth.
- Project reports include project status reports and minutes from previous meetings, lessons learned, closure reports, and other documents from all the process outputs throughout the project.
- Project presentations involve presenting project information to the stakeholders and other appropriate parties when necessary.
- Project records include memos, correspondence, and other documents concerning the project.
- Feedback received from the stakeholders that may improve future performance on projects may be captured and documented.
- Lessons learned may include positive and negative lessons.
- Managing stakeholder expectations is the process of communicating and working with stakeholders to meet their needs, addressing issues as they occur.
- An issue log or action-item log may be used to document and monitor the resolution of issues.
- A change log is used to document changes that occur during the project.
- Monitoring and controlling the project focuses on measuring project performance to identify variances from the project plan and get the project back on track.
- Monitoring the project includes collecting, measuring, and distributing project information and assessing measurements and trends to effect project improvement.
- Control includes determining corrective or preventive actions or re-planning and following up on action plans to determine if the actions taken resolved the performance issue.
- A change request may be issued as a result of comparing planned results to actual results.

- Change requests may include corrective action, preventive action, and defect repair.
- Changes may come about as a result of requests made by stakeholders.
- A change request should always be made in writing.
- Approved change requests may require new or revised cost estimates, activity sequences, schedule dates, resource requirements, and analysis of risk-response alternatives.
- Change control is focused on identifying, documenting, and controlling changes to the project and the product baselines.
- Verifying scope formally accepts completed deliverables and obtains sign-off that the deliverables are satisfactory and meet the stakeholder, customer, or sponsor's expectations.
- Scope verification is primarily concerned with acceptance of the deliverables.
- Project scope describes the work that is required to produce the product, service, or result of the project.
- The product description includes the characteristics, features, and functionality of the product, service, or result.
- Any modification to the agreed-upon work-breakdown structure is considered a scope change.
- Change to the product scope requires change to the project scope as well.
- Unapproved or undocumented changes that sometimes make their way into the project are referred to as scope creep.
- Little changes add up and eventually impact budget, schedule, and quality.

Control Scope, Schedule and Costs

- Scope control is the process of monitoring the status of the project and product and managing changes to the scope baseline.
- When scope changes are requested, you should investigate all areas of the project to determine what the changes will impact.

- Always remember to update the stakeholders regarding the changes that are being implemented and their impacts.
- Controlling the schedule is the process of monitoring the status of your project to update the project's progress and manage changes to the schedule baseline.
- Performance reviews measure, compare, and analyze schedule performance, such as actual start and finish dates, percent complete, and remaining duration for work in progress.
- An important part of schedule control is to determine whether schedule variation requires corrective action.
- An important aspect of project control includes determining the cause and degree of variance relative to the schedule baseline and deciding whether corrective or preventive action is required.
- Controlling costs is the process of monitoring the status of the project to update the project budget and manage changes to the cost baseline.
- Any increase in the authorized budget can only be approved through the integrated change control process.
- Earned-value management helps to clearly see objectively where the project is and where it is going, compared to where it was supposed to be and where it was supposed to be going.

Report Performance and Control Risks

- Project performance is the process where the collection of baseline data occurs and is documented and reported.
- You may report this information to project team members, the management team, and other interested parties.
- Reporting may include information concerning project quality, costs, scope, schedule, procurement, and risk.
- Performance reports may be presented in the form of status reports, progress measurements, or forecasts.
- Performance reports need to provide information at an appropriate level for each audience.

- The project management plan is a great source of data for performance reporting, as it provides information on project baselines.
- Information on project activities that is collected on performance results, such as deliverable status, schedule progress, and cost that are incurred, may be used for performance reporting.
- Work-performance information is used to generate project-activity metrics to evaluate progress compared to planned progress.
- You may use budget-forecast information from cost control as a source of data on project performance.
- Some project considerations are influenced by the internal organization in which the project operates.
- Performance reports organize and summarize the information gathered and present the results of any analysis compared to the performance-measurement baseline.
- Monitoring and controlling risks involve implementing response plans, tracking and monitoring identified risks, and identifying and responding to new risks as they occur.
- You should continually monitor the project work for new, changing, and outdated risks.
- Monitoring and controlling risks may involve choosing alternative strategies, executing a contingency or fallback plan, taking corrective action, and modifying the project management plan.

Applying to the Next Project

Discussion Questions

1. What is included as a part of acquiring the project team?
2. Why is it important to have completed the human resources plan during the planning process?
3. What information should be included as a part of the human resources plan?
4. What kind of information from the external environment may impact your ability to acquire the right staff for the project?

5. What should you do if you are unable to acquire the staff that you initially requested for the project?
6. What are the similarities and differences between techniques such as preassignment, negotiation, and acquisition that are used when acquiring the project team?
7. Why is it important to create the right kind of environment in terms of rewarding and recognizing the project team?
8. How important is it to align rewards and recognition to the individual's as well as to the organization's values?
9. Why is it important to ensure that project information is properly distributed?
10. What is the purpose of a performance report?
11. Why may communication skills be even more important to a project manager than technical skills?
12. Why is it necessary to have more than one method of information exchange?
13. How does the size of the group make a difference when trying to resolve conflict?
14. What are some ways that project information may be distributed?
15. How can the lessons-learned document be used to benefit future projects?
16. Why should managing stakeholder expectations be a concern to a project manager?
17. How can issues and changes be managed on a project?
18. What would happen if you did not monitor and control the project work?
19. What is the difference between monitoring a project and controlling the project? Why is it important that both of these are done?
20. How and why do changes come about on projects?
21. What are some questions that you may ask yourself once a change request is submitted?
22. What things should you consider as they relate to changes on a project?
23. What are some requirements for approved changes?

24. What are some change-management activities that are included as a part of performing integrated change control?
25. What is a configuration-management system?
26. What does the process of verifying scope entail?
27. Why is scope verification important?
28. Why is it important to control scope on a project?
29. What is involved in controlling scope on a project?
30. What does any modifications to the agreed-upon work-breakdown structure be interpreted as?
31. What term is used to refer to uncontrolled changes in a project?
32. Why should you update the stakeholders regarding the changes that are being implemented and their impacts?
33. What is defined as schedule control?
34. Why are performance reviews important as they relate to schedule control?
35. What is variance analysis, and why is it used?
36. What is the key to effective cost control?
37. What components are included as part of project costs?
38. What is the definition of earned value?
39. What kinds of questions can earned value answer?
40. Why should you be concerned about the project's performance report?
41. What information should be included as a part of the project's performance report?
42. What formats may project-performance reports take?
43. What information may be obtained from the project management plan that may be used in the project-performance report?
44. Why is work-performance information good to use when reporting on the project's performance?
45. What is meant by work-performance measurement?
46. Where would you get budget-forecast information that you may need as a part of project-performance reporting?
47. What are some project considerations that are influenced by the internal organization as they relate to project-performance reporting?

48. What is included as a part of monitoring and controlling risks?
49. Why should you monitor and control risks in a project?

Debrief Questions

1. What are the key learning points?
2. What information was new to you?
3. What concepts will you apply in the future? When?
4. What challenges do you anticipate may limit your ability to apply the concepts?
5. What needs to be in place to overcome these challenges?
6. Who would you recommend these concepts to and why?

Activity

The following activity may be completed individually or in a small group to assess your comprehension.

1. Answer the discussion questions.
2. Answer the debrief questions.
3. Use the completed template formats presented in the chapter to create documents to monitor and control a project of your own.
4. Review previous projects where monitor and controlling documents were inaccurate or not comprehensive. Discuss the outcome in those instances.

Chapter 4

Celebrate

After studying this chapter, you should be able to accomplish the following:

- explain what is meant by administering procurements
- state why administering procurements is required as a part of closing a project
- list and describe the two things that are required to close a project or phase
- list and describe the four formal types of project endings

"You can't ... you can't see the boss right now," the personal assistant splutters as the project team led by David sails past her desk. "He's preparing for a conference call and—"

David laughs aloud. "All the better," he says.

They barge into the boss's office and find him sitting at his desk, head buried deep in paper. It only takes a couple of seconds for his face to reflect the realization of what's up.

Debbie and Yvette seem to freeze momentarily. Then David steps forward, leaning over the boss's desk. "Tell me something," he says. "How do the words 'in scope, on time, and on budget' sound to you?"

The boss doesn't say a word but just glares up at David and the project team. Suddenly, he snaps out of his state of shock and jumps up from his chair. "What did you say? What?"

"Show him the evidence, Debbie. Go ahead." David says with excitement.

"Sure. Good idea."

"Is it worth it?" The boss queries.

"It sure is. At the end of this fiscal year you'll get a promotion for this project for sure, boss."

Later that evening at an exclusive restaurant perched on a cliff high above the city the project team celebrates. If the boss had any idea how much this evening cost he would surely choke on the champagne bubbles. Oh well, this is a special occasion.

"Here's to success, freedom, and a good night's sleep." Debbie lifts her champagne flute in a toast to David. "And to your continued career in project management."

Greg, the owl, the boss, Yvette, and the rest of the project team raise their flutes, toasting David. "May goliaths everywhere quake in their boots. King David rules the world of project management."

"The world's a safer place," the boss adds.

"You jokers!" David retorts, grinning broadly in spite of himself; his spirits considerably lifted. This is a special occasion.

David activates the out-of-office message to inform anyone who tries to reach him by e-mail or telephone that he is out of office on holiday for two weeks with no access to e-mails. All messages are referred to the boss until his return.

David shuts down his personal computer, packs up his desk, and is officially on holiday—a well-deserved holiday at that. The project is over; evaluations are in; project-closure documents are in place. By all accounts, the initiative is a success; but it was not accomplished without mental and physical toll. Who cares? It's over for now. David is out of office. He couldn't be more overjoyed!

Close Your Project

Before he leaves, though, David signs off on some work and cuts some checks for work completed as a part of the project and product requirements.

Administering procurements is the process of monitoring vendors' performance and ensuring that all the requirements of the contracts are met. When multiple vendors are providing goods and services to the project, administering procurements involves coordinating the interfaces among all vendors as well as administering each of the contracts. Both the buyer and the seller must administer the procurement contract for similar purposes. Each ensures that both parties meet their contractual obligations and that their own legal rights are protected.

The process of administering procurements ensures that the seller's performance meets procurement requirements and that the buyer performs according to the terms of the legal contract. The legal nature of contractual relationships makes it imperative that the project management team is aware of the legal implications of actions taken when administering any procurement.

Administering procurements includes application of the appropriate project management processes to the contractual relationship(s) and integration of the outputs from these processes into overall management of the project. The integration will occur at multiple levels when there are multiple sellers and multiple products, services, or results involved.

The project management processes that are applied may include and are not limited to the following:

- Direct and manage project execution—to authorize the seller's work at the appropriate time.
- Report performance—to monitor contract scope, cost, schedule, and technical performance,
- Perform quality control—to inspect and verify the adequacy of the seller's product,
- Perform integrated change control—to assure that changes are properly approved and that all those with a need to know are aware of such changes.
- Monitor and control risk—to ensure that risks are mitigated.

Administering procurements also has a financial management component that involves monitoring payments to the seller. This ensures that payment terms defined within the contract are met and that the seller's compensation is linked to seller progress as defined in the contract.

One of the principal concerns when making payments to suppliers is that there is a close relationship between the payments made and the work accomplished. When administering procurements, review and document how well a seller is performing or has performed based on the contract and establish corrective actions when needed.

This performance review may be used as a measure of the seller's competency for performing similar work on future projects. Similar evaluations are also carried out when it is necessary to confirm that a seller is not meeting the contractual obligations and when the buyer contemplates corrective action.

Administering procurements includes managing any early terminations of the contracted work in accordance with the termination clause of the contract. Some reasons for early termination include termination for cause, convenience, or default.

Contracts may be amended at any time prior to contract closure by mutual consent, in accordance with the change-control terms of the contract. Such amendments may not always be equally beneficial to both the seller and the buyer. Two actions are required to close a project:

1. Close the project or phase.
2. Close procurements.

When closing the project or phase, finalize all activities across all of the project management process groups to formally complete the project or phase. When closing the project, David, as project manager will review all prior information from the previous phase closures, ensuring that all project work is complete and that the project has met its objectives.

Since project scope is measured against the project management plan, as project manager David reviews that document ensuring completion before considering the project closed.

The probability of completing the project is highest during this process and risk is lowest. Stakeholders have the least amount of influence during the closing processes, while project managers have the greatest amount of influence. Costs are significantly lower during this process because the majority of the project work and spending has already occurred.

In the event that the project is terminated before completion, document the reasons for the action taken. This includes all of the activities necessary for administrative closure of the project or phase, including step-by-step methods that address

- actions and activities necessary to satisfy completion or exit criteria for the phase or project;
- actions or activities necessary to transfer the project's products, services, or results to the next phase or to production or operations; and
- activities needed to collect project or phase records, audit project success or failure, gather lessons learned, and archive project information for future use by the organization.

Projects come to an end for several reasons:

- They are successfully completed.
- They are cancelled or killed prior to completion.
- They evolve into ongoing operations and no longer exist as projects.

Four Formal Types of Project Endings

There are four formal types of project endings: addition; starvation; integration; and extinction.

Addition
Projects that evolve into ongoing operations are considered projects that end because of addition. In other words, they become an ongoing business unit. When a project becomes an ongoing operation, it is no longer a project.

Starvation
When resources are cut off from the project or are no longer provided to the project, it is starved prior to completing all the requirements. Resource starving may include cutting back or withholding human

resources, equipment and supplies, or money. The variety of reasons for starvation include the following:

- other projects come about and take precedence over the current project, thereby cutting the funding or resources for your project
- the customer curtails the order
- the project budget is reduced
- a key resource quits

Integration

Integration occurs when the resources of the project—people, equipment, property, and supplies—are distributed to other areas in the organization or are assigned to other projects.

Extinction

This is the best kind of project end, because extinction means that the project has been completed and accepted by the stakeholders. As such, it no longer exists, because it had a definite ending date, the goals of the project were achieved, and the project was closed out.

The key activity that the closed-project or closed-phase process is concerned with is gathering project records and disseminating information to formalize acceptance of the product, service, or result as well as to perform project closure. Review the project documents ensuring that they are up-to-date. For example, perhaps some scope-change requests were implemented that changed some characteristics of the final product. The project information that is collected during this process should reflect the characteristics and specifications of the final product.

Updating some resource assignments may also be necessary. Some team members will have come and gone over the course of the project. Double-check to see that the resources and their roles and responsibilities are noted.

Once the project outcome is documented, request formal acceptance from the stakeholders or the customers. The stakeholders or the customers are also interested in knowing whether the product or service of the project meets the goals that the project set out to accomplish. If the documentation is up-to-date, have the project results at hand to share with them.

The closed-project or closed-phase process is also concerned with analyzing the project management processes to determine their effectiveness and to document lessons learned concerning the project processes. Another key function of the closed-project or closed-phase process is to archive all project documents for historical reference. The closed project or phase belongs to the integration management knowledge area, because this process touches so many areas of the project.

The two results of closing a project or phase include the following:

- final product, service, or result transition
- organizational process assets update

Final product, service, or result transition refers to the transition of the final product, service, or result that the project was authorized to produce. In the case of phase closure, final product, service, or result transition refers to the intermediate product, service, or result of that phase. Otherwise, final product, service, or result transition refers to the acceptance of the final product, service, or result and the turning over of the product to the organization.

This usually requires a final sign-off or receipt indicating acceptance of the project. Formal acceptance includes distributing notice of the acceptance of the product or service of the project by the stakeholders, customer, or project sponsor. Final sign-off should be required, indicating that those signing accept the product of the project.

There are a number of organizational processes that are updated as a result of the closed-project or closed-phase process outlined below.

Project Files
Examples of documentation resulting from the project's activities include the project management plan, scope, cost, schedule and project

calendars, risk registers, change-management documentation, planned risk-response actions, and risk impact.

Project-Closure or Phase-Closure Documents

Project-closure or phase-closure documents consist of formal documentation that include completion of the project or phase and the transfer of the completed project or phase deliverables to others, such as an operations group or to the next phase.

During project closure, as project manager, David should review prior-phase documentation, customer-acceptance documentation from the verify-scope process, and the contract (if applicable). This is done to ensure that all project requirements are complete prior to finalizing project closure. If the project was terminated prior to completion, the formal documentation indicates why the project was terminated and formalizes the procedures for the transfer of the finished and unfinished deliverables of the cancelled project to others.

Ensure that historical information and lessons-learned information are transferred to the lessons-learned knowledge base for use by future projects or phases. This may include information on issues and risks as well as techniques that worked well that may be applied to future projects.

Key Points to Remember

- Administering procurements is the process of monitoring your vendor's performance and ensuring that all the requirements of the contracts are met.
- Both the buyer and the seller must administer the procurement contract for similar reasons. Each ensures that both parties meet their contractual obligation and that their own legal rights are protected.
- The purpose of administering procurements ensures that the seller's performance meets procurement requirements and that the buyer performs according to the terms of the legal contract.

- Administering procurements has a financial management component that involves monitoring payments to the seller.
- When administering procurements, you are required to review and document how well a seller is performing or has performed based on the contract and establish corrective actions when necessary.
- Administering procurements also includes managing any early termination of the contracted work in accordance with the termination clause of the contract.
- Two things required to close a project are to close the project or phase and to close procurements.
- When you close a project or phase, you finalize all activities across all of the project management process groups to formally complete the project or phase.
- The probability of completing the project is highest during the project-closing process and the risk is lowest.
- You should document the reason for actions taken in the event that the project is terminated before completion.
- Projects come to an end because they are successfully completed or they evolve into ongoing operations and no longer exist as projects.
- The four formal types of project endings are addition, starvation, integration, and extinction.
- The key activity that the closed-project or closed-phase process is concerned with is gathering project records and disseminating information to formally accept the product, service, or result as well as to perform project closure.
- Once the project outcome is documented, you will request formal acceptance from the stakeholders or the customers.
- The two results of closing a project or phase include final product, service, or result transition and updating the organizational process assets.
- During project closure, the project manager should review prior-phase documentation, customer-acceptance documentation from the verify-scope process, and the contact (if applicable).

This is done to ensure that all project requirements are completed prior to finalizing project closure.

Applying to the Next Project

Discussion Questions

1. Why should both the buyer and the seller administer the procurement contract?
2. What is the purpose of administering procurements?
3. What does the financial aspect of administering procurements entail?
4. What should be a principal concern when making payments to suppliers?
5. When can contracts be amended in a project?
6. What are two things required to close a project?
7. What does closing a project or phase entail?
8. What are some characteristics common to all projects during the closing process?
9. What should you do in the event that the project is terminated before completion?
10. Why do projects come to an end?
11. What are four formal types of project endings?
12. What is the key activity that the closed project or closed phase is concerned with?
13. What are the two results of closing a project or phase?
14. What must the project manager do during the project-closure process?

Debrief Questions

1. What are the key learning points?
2. What information was new to you?
3. What concepts will you apply in the future? When?
4. What challenges do you anticipate may limit your ability to apply the concepts?

5. What needs to be in place to overcome these challenges?
6. Who would you recommend these concepts to and why?

Activity

The following activity can be completed individually or in a small group to assess your comprehension.

1. Answer the discussion questions.
2. Answer the debrief questions.
3. Review previous project-closure documents. Discuss the outcome in those instances where the project-closure documents were inaccurate or not comprehensive.

Summary

An organization is an interactive system comprising various interrelated divisions, departments, groups, and individuals. Organizations are interactive, dynamic, and alive.

The project that David is recruited to manage is born of the need to realize organizational strategic requirements managed in the context of existing cultural norms and values.

David joins the project operating in somewhat of a vacuum. While he realizes at the outset that his networking and relationship-building skills are underdeveloped, he soon accepts that managing projects is more about people than about processes. Beginning with his first after-hour social, throughout the course of the project he is introduced to diverse networks. From his coaching sessions with the owl and one-on-one tutoring with Greg, he understands that the processes for completing the project are realized through leveraging networks. David's socialization early in the project is a turning point in his development and a key takeaway to use as a best practice when managing projects.

With no prior experience to use as his strength, David recognizes his vulnerability and uses this as impetus to develop skill in managing processes, people, and the personality conflict between Debbie and Yvette.

David's journey exposes us to practical, easy-to-use, and easy-to-understand tools and techniques that empower him to reduce feelings of anxiety and truly manage people and processes, another key takeaway from this book.

Given the increasing focus on the need for enhanced efficiencies and cost effectiveness, bringing a project in on time, in scope, and within budget is of increasing importance to organizations and individuals. *Project Management at Work* is included as a part of a learning program that provides you with the expertise to do just that.

Chapter 5 introduces you to some simple cases that you may use to continue to practice the concepts presented.

Chapter 5

Cases in Project Management

A Guide to Case Analysis

Objectives of Case Analysis

Using cases to practice project management concepts is a powerful way to accomplish the following:

- Increase your understanding of what the project manager should and should not do in the context of managing projects from initiating to closing.
- Get valuable practice with initiating, planning, executing, monitoring, controlling, and closing projects.
- Enhance your sense of business judgment.

Case discussions are not generally intended to produce concrete answers. Instead, case discussions usually produce good arguments for more than one course of action. There are often several feasible courses of action and approaches that may be used in any given scenario. The objective of case analysis is to think actively, offer analysis, propose action plans, and explain and defend the assessment.

Preparing for Case Discussion

The following approach may be used when preparing for case discussions.

1. **Read the Case**
   Reading over the case introduces you to the situation and the issue(s) involved.

2. **Decide on the Issues**

   Identify the strategic issues and problems in the case to determine what to analyze, what are the essential inputs, which tools and techniques are required, and what are the expected outputs. At times, the strategic issues are clear. At other times, You may have to dig the information out from what is presented.

3. **Use the Necessary Inputs, Tools and Techniques, and Outputs**

   Effective project management based on the framework and standards of the Project Management Institute and the *PMBOK Guide* best practices is not merely a collection of opinions; rather, it entails application of a significant number of inputs, tools and techniques, and outputs to respective knowledge areas and process groups.

   Applying the proper knowledge of project management methodology in this way cuts beneath the surface and produces important insight and understanding of strategic situations.

4. **Consider Conflicting Opinions**

   Contradictory opinions and views often surface during case discussions. This forces the analyst to develop skill in inference and judgment. A great many managerial situations entail opposing points of view, conflicting trends, and sketchy information.

5. **Support Your Diagnosis and Opinions with Reasons and Evidence**

   It is important that the analyst prepare for the question "Why?" For example, if after reviewing the case you are of the opinion that the project manager or the functional manager should act in a certain way, prepare to support your diagnosis and opinions with reasons and evidence.

6. **Develop an Appropriate Plan and Set of Recommendations**
   It is important to convert sound analysis into sound actions that are intended to produce the desired results. The final and most telling step in preparing a case is to develop an action agenda for management that lays out a set of specific recommendations on what to do. The analyst should be prepared to argue why their recommendations are more attractive than other courses of action that may be open.

Participating in Class Discussions

The following list outlines what to expect in the classroom-discussion environment:

- Expect that learners will dominate the discussion and do most of the talking. The case method requires maximum individual participation in class discussion. Being present as a silent observer throughout the entire period of time allocated for class discussion will not produce the desired result for the learner or their peers.
- Expect the instructor/facilitator to assume the role of extensive questioner and objective listener.
- Be prepared for the instructor/facilitator to probe for reasons and supporting detail based on analysis.
- Expect challenges and opposing views to those expressed as learners submit their conclusions for scrutiny and rebuttal. Learning to respect the views and approaches of others is integral to case-analysis exercises.
- Remember that it is all right to change your mind about your initial views, assumptions, and conclusions as the discussion unfolds.
- Expect to learn a lot from each case discussion. Use what you learn to be better prepared for the next case discussion and on-the-job application.

Additional Tips for Case Discussions

The following is a list of tips that may be used during case discussions:

- Do not hesitate to discuss the case before and after class with your peers. Developing effective communication skills is critical to the success as a project manager. Managers often discuss their case scenarios with others to refine their own thinking.
- Make a conscious effort to participate in case discussions rather than merely talking. Ensure that your comments add value to and build the discussion.
- Always prepare good notes for each case and refer to your notes if necessary during your presentation.

Preparing a Written Case Analysis

There is no standard procedure for preparing a written case analysis; at the same time, there are some general guidelines that may be useful. These guidelines are presented in three steps: identification, analysis and evaluation, and recommendations.

Step 1—Identification
Provide a sharply focused diagnosis of strategic issues and key problems early on in your paper. Demonstrate a clear understanding of the company's present state. Make sure that you can identify the strategy and articulate whatever strategy-implementation issues may exist.

Begin your discussion with a summary of the company's situation, its strategy, and the significant problems and issues that confront management. State problems and/or issues as precisely as you can.

Step 2—Analysis and Evaluation
Determine if the company's strategy is producing satisfactory results and determine the reasons why or why not. Determine the need for and/or the results of a needs analysis. Determine the need for project initiation. State the tasks in the respective knowledge areas and process

groups in addition to the respective inputs, tools and techniques, and outputs that will be used from project initiation to closure.

Introduce evidence to support your conclusions. Do not rely on overgeneralizations or unsupported opinion. Use tables and/or charts to present the quantitative analysis. Demonstrate the use of the concepts and analytical tools incorporated in the project management discipline.

Make sure that the interpretation of the data in the case study is reasonable and objective. Be careful to present a balanced argument.

Step 3—Recommendations

The final section of the written case analysis should consist of a set of definite recommendations along with an action plan. Recommendations should address all of the problems/issues identified and analyzed. Check to see if your recommendations are workable in terms of acceptance by the persons involved and the organization's ability to implement them.

Case 1
PJ Enterprises

PJ Enterprises is a mail-order catalog business that has been in operation for the past six years. The company develops, manufactures, and markets high-quality gifts, apparel, and home accessories and distributes them through its mail-order catalog and its retail store. The company focuses on the needs of women between the ages of twenty-five and fifty-five who own their own homes and have family incomes between forty thousand and eighty thousand dollars. PJ Enterprises believes that female catalog shoppers look for traditional, nostalgic, and romantic gifts, apparel, and home accessories to enhance the quality of their homes and family lives.

PJ Enterprises' catalog offerings include sweaters, skirts, and novelty items. Unique jewelry such as pins, earrings, belts, necklaces, and bracelets are also included in the catalog. Children's products including puzzles and toys for children ages two to ten as well as lamps, rugs, and other accessories to bring traditional or nostalgic appearance to children's rooms are also found in the catalog. The catalog also includes evergreen wreaths, centerpieces, collectable handcraft figurines, plates, dolls, and other inspirational and symbolic items reflecting traditional values.

At present, the catalog division of PJ Enterprises is located in a building that has four thousand square feet of office space and six thousand square feet of warehouse space. The company pays about five thousand dollars per month in principal and interest for the use of the space.

PJ Enterprises recorded a profit for this year with annual sales of six million dollars. Despite the recession, high points for this year included the following:

- increase of 31 percent in catalog customer lists to 250,000 names
- increase of 41 percent in sales
- net profit of one million dollars for this fiscal year

Business Plan Goals

The management team of PJ Enterprises is presently negotiating the business plan for the upcoming year. Some concerns expressed include whether it is reasonable to expect that the company will continue to grow at the present rate. If so, could the present management team facilitate and control the growth while remaining profitable? Where should the company grow? How will this be achieved? What financial, human resources and other resources would be required?

Last Year's Targets	This Year's Targets
$5 million in annual sales	$7 million in annual sales
$10 million in catalog sales	$13 million in catalog sales
$5 million from the retail division	$7 million from the retail division
$10 million from acquisitions	$12 million from acquisitions
21 percent increase in customer lists	40 percent increase in customer lists
Net profit of $1 million	Net profit of $2 million

Business Objectives

- Grow aggressively to maintain or exceed projected targets.
- Maintain profitability.
- Focus on quality and customer service with 10 percent improvement on customer service scores.
- Focus on quality of work environment and staff development and recognition.

The company estimates that capital expenditures of four hundred thousand to five hundred thousand dollars would be needed to increase catalog sales to the thirteen million dollar mark. There is also a need to increase the company's customer list. The larger the house list, the less need there is for the company to rent other lists. As the house list grows, promotional costs decrease as net sales increase. The company can also earn money from the rental of its own house list.

Organization and Staffing

PJ Enterprises' catalog division presently employs fifty people. Forty staff members are employed on a full-time basis. Included in the number of employees are four customer service supervisors and twenty-five telephone operators.

The catalog director, Judie Thompson, is responsible for all aspects of the catalogs. This year for the first time the company produced four different catalogs—one for each season. Previously, the summer catalog was essentially the spring catalog with sale prices. The spring catalog, featuring Easter gift items, was forty pages and was mailed in the end of December. The summer catalog was thirty-two pages and was mailed in mid-April. The forty-page fall catalog featured Halloween, Thanksgiving, and some Christmas items and was mailed in the end of June. The biggest-ever Christmas catalog was forty-eight pages and was mailed in mid-September.

Sheena Perez, the merchandising manager, is responsible for selecting and promoting items for the catalogs. Sheena and Judie frequent gift, apparel, and other trade shows throughout the year, seeking vendors with quality products and reputation for reliability in shipping. They bring potential catalog items back to the office where they, along with the assistant merchandising manager, examine each piece and argue for or against offering it to the PJ Enterprises catalog customers.

After the catalog merchandise is selected, Sheena Perez works closely with a contract copywriter and professional service firms contracted to design and produce the catalog, including layout, photography, and printing. The vendor-selection process includes interviewing, negotiating, inspecting, and managing. Before the catalogs are mailed, the customer service supervisors and the telephone operators are trained on each catalog item. This training is conducted by Sheena Perez, the merchandising manager, and Judie Thompson, the catalog director.

This half-day training is conducted using a PowerPoint presentation method. Thirty minutes are reserved at the end of the meeting for questions and answers. Training materials include a summary product description for easy reference on the automated-entry system. Product-catalog training is conducted four times per year just prior to the introduction of the new season's catalog.

Thus far, the company has rotated more than five hundred products through its catalogs over the six years that it has been in operation.

Quality and Service

PJ Enterprises has a goal of quality service delivery. The company has a toll-free telephone number for placing orders and for customer service inquiries and complaints. Its present telephone system can support twenty incoming lines and forty headsets and has automatic call-distribution features and activity-reporting capability. The results of a brief customer service survey that the telephone operators are required to conduct with every customer are also captured as a part of the activity reporting. Telephone operators can access product-reference guides and answer questions while the customer is on the line.

The phone lines are staffed twenty-four hours per day, seven days per week. The telephone operators answer telephone calls using the standard greeting, place the order directly on the system, and encourage the customer to answer a few brief customer service questions. If the customer requires service, the telephone operator transfers the call to the customer service supervisor on duty. The present system is designed to answer 90 percent of all customer inquiries within two minutes and to ensure that the customer is kept happy. At the moment, the telephone system is only used at 85 percent capacity.

Reports generated by the system indicate that each telephone operator only responds to three calls per hour as opposed to the required number of six calls per hour. Customer service data reveal that two customers out of every three who respond to the customer service survey have a complaint about the telephone operator. Complaints are typically around product knowledge, telephone etiquette, and prompt response to calls waiting in the queue. Customers complain that even after the long wait to speak to a telephone operator, they are asked to call back or are redirected to a customer service supervisor to have their query answered satisfactorily. Fifty percent of the customers surveyed from last year responded that they are not inclined to do business with PJ Enterprises again as a result of the poor customer service that they received.

The average order is between $250 and $500, so revenue is generated by call volume and sales volume. Customer benefits include competitive prices, optional overnight delivery, and quick shipping from receipt of order.

PJ Enterprises stresses the importance of quality in all aspects of the work, from producing the catalog to taking, packing, and shipping an order. Incentives are awarded for both warehouse and customer service staff for error-free performance.

Issues for Management

- Upgrade of current hardware configuration with additional work stations as well as new equipment and technical improvement in the warehouse is necessary for the projected increase in catalog sales.
- Human resources challenges continue to be a concern for the company's management team. One of the greatest challenges is recruiting, selecting, hiring, training, and managing new people. There is a high turnover of staff on all levels, particularly with the telephone operators, customer service supervisors, and warehouse staff. On average, one staff member resigns or is terminated every other month.
- Just recently, some new HR policies were introduced to the staff. These policies include a performance-evaluation/self-evaluation process, a new company handbook, and an upgrade to the company's pension plan.
- Employee meetings are now scheduled to be held once per month but often are very poorly attended because of the employees' working hours. Employees are not compensated for attending these meetings.

- Customer-survey figures indicate an increase of 30 percent in customer complaints with the telephone operators as compared to the same period in the previous year.
- More than half of the total number of telephone operators were informally interviewed and indicated dissatisfaction with their jobs to the point of leaving.

Practical Exercise

In light of the aggressive targets and alleged employee dissatisfaction among telephone operators in particular, senior management is proposing the use of a slightly different approach for the training that is typically conducted before the catalog mailing.

As project manager, you are hired by PJ Enterprises to manage a project intended to design, develop, and deliver a learning program for the telephone operators. The training course is intended to be delivered before the catalogs are mailed.

The target audience is the customer service supervisors and the telephone operators. Participants are to be trained on each catalog item. The project is to create the course to design, develop, and deliver training that will replace the training course that was previously conducted by Sheena Perez, the merchandising manager, and Judie Thompson, the catalog director.

Management believes that an increase in knowledge and skill in describing the features and benefits of the products in the catalog is necessary to increase catalog sales and reduce customer complaints.

A budget of four hundred thousand dollars is allocated for all staff training during the upcoming the fiscal year.

Review the details in the case presented above and consider how you may use your knowledge and skill in project management to address the situation above.

Use the data provided in the case to complete all project management documents that you recommend be completed as a part of this case analysis. Submit these documents, along with your written case findings, for grading.

Case 2
Mama's Home-Renovation Project

As Mama ages, her children become increasingly concerned about her physical safety. Mama has lived independently for years. That's before crime statistics began reflecting an average of one murder per day and heaven only knows how many armed robberies, attempted armed robberies, house break-ins, and other petty crime.

Last year the family convinced Mama to install a house alarm system. This installation addresses the immediate security issue, but what about other components of safety and security? Perhaps the burden of the concern lies with Mama's children, who believe that more should be done to prepare for her eventual move out of the "family homestead" and relocation into the home of one of her children.

The children are prepared to pool their financial resources to convert a slanted-roof garage and washroom attached to her son's residence to comfortable living quarters for Mama. This 240-square-foot area will be converted into three main living areas: a kitchen/sitting room area, a bedroom, and a bathroom. The renovation project must comply with all local building codes and standards.

Requirements for Project Manager

As project manager, you are required to conduct a needs analysis to determine what, if any, special requirements are needed to accommodate Mama. Determine whether special permits or inspections are required for the project and whether there are any fees or costs that will not be covered by the contractor. You are also expected to complete a thorough estimation of construction materials and supplies.

The total project budget is set at thirty thousand dollars (inclusive of contingency allowances reserved for known risks). The project is expected to be completed in three months. Furniture is out of scope for this project.

Review the details in the case presented above and consider how you may use your knowledge and skill in project management to address the situation above.

Use the data provided in the case to complete all project management documents that you recommend be completed as a part of this case analysis. Submit these documents, along with your written case findings, for grading.

Case 3
Liz and Jim Takeout

Liz and Jim Takeout has been in operation for the past three years. The menu features fried chicken, fried fish, fried pork chops, hot dogs, hamburgers, French fries, and fountain sodas. Liz and Jim McKenzie started the business with little more than their life savings and a dream of success. Neither of them had extensive background in business or restaurant operations.

The initial investment was approximately $315,000. The majority of the funds were for land and a building, which averaged $200,000. The equipment investment was about $85,000, and working capital requirements were about $30,000.

Liz and Jim's first order of business was to hire a professional kitchen designer, who created a unique kitchen layout designed for fast and efficient service. The kitchen layout is very efficient in everything from storage to inventory control, cooking efficiency, and order delivery.

Liz and Jim's business strategy was to do everything as simply as possible and avoid sophisticated accounting systems and legal agreements. As Liz and Jim Takeout grew in popularity, so did the number of persons on staff. Head count swelled from three persons in the first year of business to thirty persons. The rapid expansions seemed to be getting out of hand. Liz and Jim wasted no time in hiring persons for the store, most of whom were members of their direct or extended family. In recent months, there has been quarreling among some family members. This has impacted sales, service, and overall staff morale.

Jim McKenzie has always been a reluctant leader who despises conflict and often feels uncomfortable in any kind of meeting, even if the audience is only a few friends. Although generally well liked by most people in the organization, Jim faces a major crisis in the business that he and his wife started. With sales, profits, and service continuing to decline, Jim McKenzie convinces Liz to agree to go outside of the company and bring in a professional manager who has no ties to the direct or extended family. In Jim McKenzie's view, housecleaning is in order and special management talent is needed.

Six months ago, Bradshaw Hamilton, a professional manager, was brought in to turn the company around. Bradshaw's initial assessment of the company revealed the following information.

- The company is not profitable.
- No management strategies, goals, or plans are in place.
- The company's image is old and faded.
- The company is not advertising.
- The company is not training its employees.
- No money is reinvested into the company.
- There is no formal system of communication in place.

Customers

For the first time in the company's history, market research is conducted. Results from the research are as follows.

- Typical customers are females between the ages of eighteen and twenty-four.
- The annual income of customers is ten to fifteen thousand dollars.
- The typical customer is a blue-collar worker and a member of a three- or four-person household.
- Sixty percent of Liz and Jim's business is done during lunchtime.
- Thirty percent of Liz and Jim's business is done during supper time.
- Ten percent of Liz and Jim's business is conducted during other periods.
- The average cost of a meal (excluding drink) is US$4.50, compared to the industry average of US$5.00 for fast food.

Training

Training in food preparation and service delivery is typically done informally and on the job by the cook. The recommendation is that formal operating manuals be designed and developed covering storage, preparation of menu items, order taking, cleaning, maintaining equipment, and customer service.

Requirements for Project Manager

Review the details of the case presented above and consider how you may use your knowledge and skill in project management to address the situation.

Use the data provided in the case to complete all project management documents that you recommend be completed as a part of this case analysis. Submit these documents, along with your written case findings, for grading.

Case 4
The International Company

You are an instructional designer employed by a large, multimillion-dollar organization with divisions in fifty-five countries in Latin America and the Caribbean. You work in a training department at the company's headquarters along with a team of seven instructional design managers. The team of instructional designers is managed by a senior manager of training.

The senior manager has been employed with the organization for twenty-five consecutive years, the last seven of which were in charge of the department to which you are assigned. The senior manager has spent all of her work life in the area of training and has been responsible for many improvements in the department since heading the training team in the company's headquarters. Achievements include the following:

- The implementation of more than thirty different e-learning modules on a variety of products and services that the company provides. These modules are used by employees in the various English- and Spanish- speaking countries where the company does business.
- The implementation of the ADDIE model as the quality standard for instructional designers in the department as well as for use by training managers in the various English- and Spanish-speaking countries where the company does business.
- The introduction of a learning management system for use within the region.
- The implementation of a number of self-study learning programs on a variety of the company's products for use within the region.

You are assigned the task by the senior manager of designing and developing two self-study learning programs to meet the company's strategic objectives, which were signed off on in the strategic plan and business plan documents. Outlined below is some important information about the present state of the department that you should be aware of.

Present State of the Department

- The company has a balanced matrix organizational structure in place.
- There is an informal project management methodology in place.
- Both learning programs are expected to be completed in a three-month period.
- No work-breakdown structure exists from previous projects, as completion of this task was not required by the senior manager.
- Your company accepts a Gantt chart format as a project plan. Your boss does not see the necessity of producing subsidiary plans as a part of a project plan.
- It is not necessary for a needs analysis to be completed in this instance, as the training is new.
- Subject matter experts from various departments in headquarters as well as throughout the region will comprise an extended project team. These persons will serve as resources for you as you progress through the project from initiation to closure.
- No formal integrated change-control structure exists from previous projects, as completion of this task was not required by the senior manager.
- No procurement process or vendor agreements will be used for this project.

Requirements for Project Manager

Review the details of the case presented above and consider how you may use your knowledge and skill in project management to address the situation.

Use the data provided in the case to complete all project management and/or instructional design documents that you recommend be completed as a part of this case analysis. Submit these documents, along with your written case findings, for grading.

Case 5
Fabulous and Fifty

Barbie is a single mother who toiled for years raising her children on her own, with sole responsibility for every bill that she and her children incurred—and there were many bills incurred over the years.

Four months from now, Barbie will be fifty years old. She wants to celebrate her birthday in grand style. Rather than doing the usual "dinner with friends in a hotel" Barbie decides to bring all of her friends and family to her home where they will celebrate with her in her backyard. She is planning to invite one hundred guests. Barbie's goal is to create an experience for her guests beginning with the appearance and distribution of the invitations. She envisions a grand affair and has more than enough space to work with. Her backyard is six thousand square feet, including a thirty-five-foot-long swimming pool, and she wants every inch of it transformed into an exotic vista. Of course she does not want her flower beds trampled, and there is an issue of security as the yard is only partially enclosed—Barbie does not want uninvited guests.

While there is a twenty-square-foot raised patio as you exit the kitchen, this will not be used for dancing; instead Barbie envisions the use of this space to address some other logistical consideration.

Barbie's budget of twenty thousand dollars will cover the costs of tables, chairs, tent(s), entertainment and lighting, décor, and a gourmet menu inclusive of drinks and hors d'oeuvres. Barbie is expecting that each table will be adorned with linen and centerpieces and that serving and janitorial services will be provided as a part of the budget. Of course, she is expecting to have prizes and surprises for her guests as well as party favors and party bags.

Requirements for Project Manager

As project manager, you are required to conduct a needs analysis to determine what, if any, special requirements are needed to meet Barbie's needs. Determine whether special permits or inspections and/

or ordinances are required to ensure the project's success and whether there are any fees or costs that will not be covered by the budget.

Review the details in the case presented above and consider how you may use your knowledge and skill in project management to address the situation.

Use the data provided in the case to complete all project management documents that you recommend be completed as a part of this case analysis. Submit these documents, along with your written case findings, for grading.

Case 6
JJ Enterprises

JJ Enterprises is a locally owned and operated fast-food restaurant in business for the past five years. As JJ Enterprises grew in popularity, so did the number of locations and persons on staff. Head count increased from three persons in the first year to eighty persons presently on staff. Locations grew from one to fifteen. The rapid expansion appears out of hand, particularly as it relates to record keeping.

Expected Performance

The following should be in place in JJ Enterprises to ensure that records are created, filed, sorted, retrieved, and/or disposed of in keeping with standard records management procedures:

- a records classification system where individual records are arranged according to either the record activity (use) or the importance of particular records or both
- a system that facilitates the proper creation, utilization, retention, transfer, and disposal of records
- written procedures for records storage and retrieval based on prescribed rules and procedures

Actual Performance

- Records are not classified as active or inactive.
- Records are not classified as vital, important, useful, or nonessential.
- No documents are in place to identify the persons with the authority to create records in JJ Enterprises.
- No system of central control of records exists to make sure that records are carefully monitored as they are created.
- No documented procedures are in place to provide instructions on the format, procedures, rationale, purpose, cost, or estimated life of a new record.

- No established filing classification and records inventory exists to assist in ensuring that the created record is used, stored, and retrieved for the purpose(s) intended.
- No system for records retention has been developed to include the process for determining active, semiactive, and inactive storage.
- No established criteria exists for transferring records from active to inactive storage depending on the record activity.
- No established process is in place for purging or destroying records that are no longer needed.
- There is no well-organized computer-assisted storage/retrieval system that takes into consideration the future expansion of JJ Enterprises as it relates to records management.
- No appropriate filing equipment for paper storage and noncorrespondence storage is in place.

Data-Collection Method
The methods used to collect needs-analysis data include

- observation;
- interview; and
- on-the-job demonstration and application.

Cause of Performance Gap
- There is no records classification system where individual records are arranged according to either the record activity (use) or the importance of particular records or both.
- There is no system that facilitates the proper creation, utilization, retention, transfer, and disposal of records.
- There are no procedures for records storage and retrieval based on prescribed rules and procedures.
- There is no well-organized computer-assisted storage/retrieval system that takes into consideration the future expansion of JJ Enterprises as it relates to records management.
- There is no appropriate filing equipment for paper storage and noncorrespondence storage.

Cost of Project

Project cost to design, develop, and implement the records storage and retrieval system at JJ Enterprises is estimated at US$30,000.

Benefit of the Project

- Create greater efficiency.
- Develop competencies within staff.
- Empower staff to improve performance based on improved systems and processes.
- Demonstrate commitment on behalf of management to develop improved working conditions for employees.
- Enhance customer service experience based on efficiency in tracking, retrieving, and following up on relevant correspondence.
- Create greater value between the organization, the employees, and the customers.

Requirements for Project Manager

As project manager, you are required to develop and implement a robust records management system inclusive of a set of documented rules based on conventional standards for records management. Immediately after implementation, the program will be measured based on the use, ease of filing, and retrieval of records as it relates to records classification and the records cycle.

Review the details in the case presented above and consider how you may use your knowledge and skill in project management to address the situation. Use the data provided in the case to complete all project management documents that you recommend be completed as a part of this case analysis. Submit these documents, along with your written case findings, for grading.

About the Author

Dorcas M. T. Cox is instructional designer and director of project services for Project Management Solutions Limited, a successful project management training and consultancy company. Project Management Solutions Limited offers a range of services while identifying and responding to your specific requirement:

- standard and customized project management courses (including Project Essentials, Project Intermediate, and PMI Certification)
- project management speakers bureau
- on- or off-site delivery of project management services
- project team meeting facilitation
- project team coaching

Dorcas combined over eighteen years of instructional design and project management expertise to earn Project Management Solutions Limited the Registered Educational Provider designation from the Project Management Institute (REP #3627), this designation indicates that the organization is approved by the Project Management Institute to offer project management training.

Dorcas has worked in government agencies as well as designed instructional material for a multinational corporation that is used in English and Spanish throughout Central America and the Caribbean. She has facilitated training sessions in Canada and throughout the Bahamas and Caribbean, including Trinidad, Barbados, Belize, and St. Lucia. She continues to work as an adjunct instructor for academic institutions. Dorcas has studied, lived, and worked in North America and Canada. She earned her Project Management Professional distinction from the Project Management Institute and presently lives in The Bahamas with her son.

She can be reached via e-mail at dorcas.cox@gmail.com. You can also learn more about the products and services offered by Project Management Solutions Limited by visiting the website: www. projectmanagementsolutionsltd.com.

Resources

Heldman, K. *PMP Project Management Professional Exam Study Guide*, 4th ed. Wiley Publishing, Hoboken NJ., 2007.

Project Management Institute. *A Guide to the Project Management Body of Knowledge (PMBOK Guide),* 5th ed. Project Management Institute, Newtown Square, Pennsylvania 2013.

www.ingramcontent.com/pod-product-compliance
Lightning Source LLC
Chambersburg PA
CBHW030933180526
45163CB00002B/557